TRANSFORMED BY THE CLEANSING
BLOOD OF
JESUS CHRIST
ALONE WHO IS THE GRACE OF GOD

TRANSFORMED BY THE CLEANSING
BLOOD OF
JESUS CHRIST
ALONE WHO IS THE GRACE OF GOD

VOLUME 2

BY GARFIELD CAMBRIDGE

ISBN: 978-1-965679-19-7 Paperback
ISBN: 978-1-965679-30-2 Ebook
ISBN: 978-1-965679-31-9 Hardback

Rev. date: 11/05/2024

CONTENTS

ACKNOWLEDGMENT

Without the help of Almighty God, I could not have maintained the focus and discipline necessary to write this book. I am convinced that it is God who has granted me the opportunity to share my experiences of discovering His nature—that which God has revealed to us so that we can know Him for who He is to mankind, for what humanity know about the all sufficient One, is a tiny fraction of His full nature that the universe and beyond cannot contain. No created thing can understand the full scope of a limitless being. This book aims to illustrate who God is and His relationship with sinful humanity. My hope is that it will guide those who have yet to know the true God—revealed through the Holy Scriptures—to discover their identity in Jesus Christ and have peace from God through Him.

The aim of the book also is to seek to assist those who have already received the gift of eternal life to examine their lives in the light of God's Word. My prayer is that God will open our spiritual eyes, helping us recognize our need for Him and encouraging us to emulate His character. For readers unfamiliar with Jesus Christ, I hope this book prompts serious consideration of the consequences of ignoring God's call. God desires for each of us to engage with His Word, where the scriptures testify about Jesus, the giver of Salvation and eternal life.

God has moved me to use my gift of writing to convey what the Bible teaches about the Gospel of Jesus Christ, whose teachings are found exclusively in the Scriptures. The gospel offers the good news of God's remedy for sin through salvation—a covenantal relationship between God and humanity. My family has been incredibly supportive and encouraging, bolstering my faith and commitment to complete this project. If we acknowledge God in all our ways and use our gifts for the benefit of Christ's body and His glory, He will guide our paths and enrich our lives with blessings as profound as those described in Ephesians 3:20.

As a child of God, I have witnessed His miraculous interventions for my family and me. In moments of turmoil and seeming impossibility, when I was overwhelmed with worry and saw no way out of my difficulties, God was my refuge. Unbeknownst to me, my grandmother's prayers on my behalf were heard and answered, leading to my deliverance from profound distress. God continues to rescue individuals from all manner of strife. He alone can liberate anyone from the depths of sin, transforming them from spiritual death into life through Jesus Christ. God stands ready to be your helper and savior if you allow Him into your life.

Throughout various trials, God has revealed His superior plan for my life. No true child of God faces trials alone, for He accompanies us through every challenge. He is a friend more loyal than any other, more reliable than even the closest confidante. Although I was once spiritually blind, God continues to open my eyes to the richness of His promises. During my reckless years, I was deaf to God's voice—His words of forgiveness, mercy, and grace. Yet, in His abundant mercy, He restored my ability to hear and comprehend the melodies of salvation and the songs of redemption. To God be the glory for the great things He has accomplished for me and countless others; He truly deserves our praise and worship.

Living according to God's ways is infinitely better than my previous worldly life. Embracing a new life in Christ is not without its challenges. Indeed, spiritual attacks often intensify after accepting Jesus Christ as Savior and Lord. Yet, despite the inner conflict between our sinful desires and the reborn spirit, and despite a world hostile to God and His commandments, living a true Christian life is challenging but achievable. As the Apostle Paul writes to the Galatians, *"I am crucified with Christ: nevertheless I live; yet not I, but Christ liveth in me: and the life which I now live in the flesh I live by the faith of the Son of God, who loved me, and gave himself for me" (Galatians 2:20).*

Thus, life is truly worth living God's way, for whom the Son sets free is free indeed. This freedom is what I longed for and could only find when the Lord called me and released the bonds of iniquity that compelled me to commit all manners of evil. God has liberated my soul from the chains of sin and the darkness that once imprisoned me. Though my family and I face trials in this world, I am assured that God is greater than any adversary, including Satan. He transcends every circumstance and is mightier than any challenge we might encounter.

God uses the tribulations we face to foster and fortify our faith in Him. My family and I constantly lean on God, trusting Him in everything and bringing our concerns to Him in prayer. God is my Creator, Redeemer, Sustainer, and the one who nourishes me with His life-giving Word while guiding me through His Holy Spirit. He is the Alpha and Omega, the beginning and the end of all things, the only wise God. There is none besides Him. Let God accomplish His perfect work in your life today.

PREFACE

The Bible is a unique book. It reveals who God—the Creator of the universe and beyond—is to humanity. It declares that God's nature is inherently just and fair, with grace and mercy permeating His actions. He endowed us with every good and perfect gift, intending that we glorify Him in all aspects of our lives. God, in His perfection, crafted mankind and the environment as masterpieces on a canvas of love for His glory, according to Genesis 1. Since God is perfect, His creations are inherently good, and He made no errors in His work.

Every person carries a mark of excellence from their Creator. Each gentle brush stroke of the Master Painter is a wonder, making every individual a sublime masterpiece. Yet, it is humanity that has chosen to spurn this divine love and care, opting instead for sin and its consequences. Ecclesiastes 7:29 reflects on this, stating, "Lo, this only I have found, that God hath made man upright; but they have sought out many inventions."

For those not yet saved, God remains an enigma, a question mark looming large. However, the Bible reveals this mystery through Jesus Christ, promising rest and peace to any sinner who seeks Him through diligent study of the Scriptures.

God extends an irresistible offer—eternal life through Jesus Christ, a gift that comes without cost. This gift is ready to be claimed. Once received, we are encouraged to share this good news with others. Choose life in God, and let His life transform yours, securing an eternal relationship with Him.

God's desire is for us to recognize His fairness and justice and to understand His generosity. He is acutely aware of the human condition—our torments and the masks we wear to hide our pain. God knows that earthly pleasures cannot fill the void within us; only He can satisfy our deepest longings. Yet, humanity has turned away, seeking fulfillment in polluted waters of sin, leading to hearts hardened by iniquity.

Jesus Christ, in His boundless patience and love, waits for us to accept the new life He offers. He is the author and finisher of our faith, the source of our salvation. But His invitation will not last indefinitely. The call to be born again is urgent—today is the day to embrace this opportunity.

God will not let us wander aimlessly on the perilous paths of sin without the chance to know Jesus Christ as our Savior and Lord. He is both the way to God and the gate to eternal life, and the path through Him is narrow.

The narrow path leading to eternal life with God is challenging, as forewarned by Matthew 7:13-14, which describes hell's ever-widening gate, contrasting sharply with the narrow gate that leads to life. This broad path, likened to the woman of Revelation 17, symbolizes spiritual Babylon, intoxicated with the blood of God's saints who chose martyrdom over sinning against their Savior and Shepherd, the Lord Jesus Christ.

Jesus emphasizes in Matthew 16:38, "For whosoever will save his life shall lose it: and whosoever will lose his life for my sake shall find it." He calls us to deny ourselves, take up our crosses, and follow Him, embodying the spirit of humility that marks God's kingdom. If you hear the voice of God beckoning you away from spiritual Babylon, follow His voice and enter through the narrow gate that is Jesus Christ.

Many churches wrongly teach multiple paths to God and deny the existence of hell. These false prophets, operating under the dominion of Satan—the dragon, the beast, and the false prophet—are masquerading as messengers of light to deceive and lead astray those who are still feeding on the milk of the Word, and those individuals that God is calling to Himself. These false teachings pave a broad way to destruction, as Satan, posing as an angel of light, tempts those wavering in their faith with promises he cannot fulfill. The reality of his deception leads only to eternal damnation.

This false Christ will assert himself in the temple of God, claiming divine authority and demanding worship, as described in 2 Thessalonians 2:4. His church, a façade of godliness, performs signs and wonders to captivate and deceive even the elect, if possible, as warned in Matthew 24:24. Yet, God's true church persists, adhering to His commandments and bearing the testimony of Jesus, stay steadfast on the narrow path by tightly holding on to the compassionate and secure hand of Almighty God.

Despite humanity's rebellion, God was willing to compromise His absolute holiness to redeem us from our sins. He temporarily set aside His divine glory and took on human flesh within the confines of time and space. Born of a virgin whom He created, and don Himself in the garments of sin cursed flesh. Thus, He said sacrifice and offering you did not desire, but a body you have prepared for me. Wherefore, the Creator of the universe and beyond confined Himself into the limitations of time in that the great I AM God was pricked in His flesh with the plight of sinful humanity. Whereby God in the Person of the Lord Jesus Christ embraced human frailty and susceptibility to temptation, identifying with our sufferings and paying the ultimate price for our redemption on the cross at Calvary. Here, Christ bore the full weight of our sins and sorrows, remaining sinless throughout His trials.

Christ's sacrificial blood cleanses the repentant sinner, affirming Him as the Lamb of God who takes away the sins of the world. This profound act of love underscores that faith comes from hearing and believing the Word of God in its entirety.

As children of God, we are called to surrender fully to His will, accepting the whole of Scripture and allowing God to guide our lives completely. This total submission is the essence of true discipleship and the path to eternal fellowship with our Creator.

To us, transforming our understanding and guiding us into all wisdom. The Scriptures stand as a divine revelation, where God communicates His will and His ways to mankind. They are not merely historical documents or moral guidebooks but are the living, active voice of God Himself, meant to penetrate our hearts and change our lives.

True faith involves embracing everything God has revealed in His Word. It is through the guidance of the Holy Spirit that we come to understand and believe what is written in the Bible. As Romans 10:17 states, "So then faith cometh by hearing, and hearing by the word of God." By accepting God's invitation to salvation, He promises to break the chains of sin that imprison us, removing the veil that separates us from His love. It is sin that keeps humanity in darkness, away from the life-giving presence of God.

God offers beauty for ashes, the oil of joy for mourning, and the garment of praise for the spirit of heaviness, as declared in Isaiah 61:1-3. This transformation is intended so that believers might be called trees of righteousness, planted by the Lord and displaying His glory in their lives.

In a world rife with chaos, true peace can be elusive. Wealth, power, influence, and prestige alone cannot secure peace of mind. Without God's intervention, these possessions end up controlling us, rather than being managed by us. True peace is not merely the absence of conflict but is the profound peace of God that calms our worries, banishes our doubts, and dispels our fears, even amidst life's storms.

Many search for peace and fulfillment in all the wrong places. They pursue relationships and achievements hoping to quench the thirst of their souls, but these are futile efforts without God. John 7:37-38 offers a divine invitation: "If any man thirst, let him come unto me, and drink. He that believeth on me, as the scripture hath said, out of his belly shall flow rivers of living water". This passage promises that those who turn to Christ will find a source of satisfaction that never runs dry.

Have your pursuits left you feeling empty and unfulfilled? Entrust your life to God, embracing all that He offers, and experience His goodness. Once you have tasted what He provides, you will no longer hunger or thirst for anything else. God's gift of salvation is complete and unending. He does not count your sins against you once forgiven; He will never let you down, forsake you, or disappoint you. God is truthful, consistently revealing the truth in His Word, even when it is difficult for us to face.

God's Word is filled with the saving truth intended for every soul. Without Jesus Christ, there is no access to God—He is the way, the truth, and the life. Jesus is the great light that dispels the darkness of unbelief and guides us to the Father.

God encourages everyone to engage with the Scriptures personally. John 5:39 and other passages throughout the Bible emphasize the importance of studying the Word diligently. Whether we are lost, out of order, or burdened by life's challenges, the Scriptures, through the Spirit of God, offer guidance, correction, and comfort, leading us back to the embrace of God, who alone can heal and restore our weary souls.

The wisdom of God may seem foolish to the natural man, as stated in 1 Corinthians 2:14, but to those who are led by the Spirit, the Scriptures reveal the profound truths of God's kingdom, making wise those who would otherwise remain in ignorance. Engage deeply with the Word of God, allow the Holy Spirit to illuminate your understanding, and discover the joy of a life fully surrendered to Him.

True faith entails believing everything God communicates through His Word. Guided by the Holy Spirit, we gain understanding and believe the scriptures, becoming wise unto righteousness. However, to the world, this divine wisdom often seems foolish because it does not comprehend God's ways.

God's approach to salvation has remained unchanged. That still small voice speaks to the heart, making one uncomfortable with their current way of living. Do not harden your heart or quench His Spirit as it pleads with you to accept the gift of eternal life—a gift we are unworthy of but is given because God so loved the world. In His immense love, He came as a man, Jesus Christ, born of a virgin, humbling Himself to become the unblemished Lamb of God, taking upon Himself the punishment for our transgressions. Christ bore God's full wrath, satisfying the debt required by divine law to absolve our sins.

God's method of seeking the lost has been consistent since the days of Adam, hiding from his sin. The Holy Scriptures have remained unchanged through millennia, despite skeptics' claims of corruption. While interpretations vary, leading to the formation of various denominations, these do not alter the Scripture itself. Cultural shifts do not change God's Word; rather, His Word changes cultures across ages.

Matthew 24:14 states, "And this gospel of the kingdom shall be preached in all the world for a witness unto all nations; and then shall the end come." Salvation is a divine gift, accessible to all, without prerequisites. God's love reaches out to everyone, calling them from darkness into His marvelous light, represented by Jesus Christ, the Savior of all who believe.

Jesus Christ illuminates the hearts of humanity with His truth, reaching across social, political, and religious divides. He calls us from the grave of sin to become vessels filled with His presence. As declared in John 8:12, "I am the light of the world. Whoever follows me will not walk in darkness, but will have the light of life." Let the light of Jesus be the spiritual change you seek.

I invite you to engage with the Bible, seeking understanding from God as you explore its pages. It is through His Word that we find peace with God and receive forgiveness for our sins. God grants the gift of repentance and offers a life of fellowship to those who do not resist His gospel. A life surrendered to Jesus Christ is transformed, profoundly and permanently changed for the better.

Jeremiah 29:12-14 promises, "Then you will call on me and come and pray to me, and I will listen to you. You will seek me and find me when you seek me with all your heart. I will be found by you", declares the Lord. God responds to those who earnestly seek Him, providing clear evidence of His goodness, wrapped in mercy and grace, guiding them to Himself.

As you read this book, "Called to be Chosen," it will direct you to the Holy Scriptures, helping you discover who God is and all He has to offer, potentially changing your life forever. Be blessed, my friend, and again I say, be blessed.

CHAPTER 11

SATAN, THE FATHER OF LIES

The armor of God is to protect His people from the wiles of the devil penetrating their lives. For Satan's desire, is to get the opportunity to steal, kill, and destroy the unsaved before they get the opportunity to hear God's Word get planted into their hearts. The armor less people are those who are still hesitating on the gospel of eternal life though salvation and faith in Jesus Christ. Their vulnerability makes them easy targets for Satan's deceptive tactics. And so Satan's ultimate aim is to keep individuals from embracing the gospel and experiencing the transformative power of Jesus Christ.

Satan is the prince of darkness. He is the prince of the power of the air, the spirit that is now working in the children of disobedience (Ephesians 2:2). He is every unsaved person's ruling authority.

Despite the pernicious influence of Satan, believers are equipped with divine tools for defense and victory. Ephesians 6:10-18 details the full armor of God, which includes the belt of truth, the breastplate of righteousness, the shield of faith, the helmet of salvation, and the sword of the Spirit, which is the Word of God. These elements are essential for standing firm against the devil's schemes and ensuring spiritual survival.

The role of prayer cannot be overstated; it is through prayer that we invoke God's strength and wisdom to resist and overcome the wiles of the devil. It is also through prayer that we ask for discernment, so we may not be deceived by Satan's subtleties. Continuous prayer helps fortify our spiritual defenses and keeps us aligned with God's will, making it harder for Satan to find a foothold.

God's sovereignty remains a beacon of hope for all believers. He has predestined a plan of salvation that no force of evil can thwart. For those who hear and respond to the call of Jesus Christ, there is the promise of redemption and eternal life, making them impervious to the ultimate harm Satan seeks to inflict.

For the unsaved, the danger is real, as Satan actively works to prevent them from seeing the truth of the gospel. However, God's call is powerful and persistent, and His grace is available to all who seek Him. The Lord continually works through His people, His Word, and His Spirit to draw more souls out of darkness and into His marvelous light.

As believers, we are urged to be vigilant and proactive in our spiritual lives. By diligently studying the scriptures and living according to God's precepts, we protect ourselves from deception. Sharing the gospel with others not only spreads the good news but also disrupts Satan's plans to keep people in bondage to sin.

And so while Satan is a formidable enemy, his power is limited compared to the sovereign authority of Almighty God. For those who are covered by the blood of Christ and armed with the truth of the scripture, Satan's attempts to destroy will ultimately fail. Therefore, let us commit to wearing the full armor of God, engaging in persistent prayer, and actively participating in the mission to spread the gospel, thus safeguarding ourselves and others from the deceptions of the enemy.

Recognizing and understanding the tactics of the enemy is crucial in maintaining spiritual health and vitality.

God, in His infinite wisdom, provides us with the necessary resources and strength to overcome these adversities. He does not leave us to face these challenges alone but is always present, guiding us through His Spirit and the Scriptures. As believers, it is essential to maintain a close relationship with God, committing time for worship and prayer, which acts as our spiritual lifeline.

By recognizing the enemy's distractions and focusing on God, we empower ourselves to withstand the devil's schemes. The power of scripture is our defense against Satan's lies. When we are well-versed in the Word, we can counteract his deceptions with truth. James 4:7 tells us to submit ourselves to God, resist the devil, and he will flee from us. This formula is not just a recommendation but a divine strategy for spiritual warfare.

Additionally, fostering a community of faith where believers support and uplift each other is vital. The collective strength of the church can repel the advances of the enemy, strengthening each member within it.

The encouragement and prayers of fellow believers are instrumental in fortifying one's faith and resilience against spiritual attacks.

As we continue to engage in this spiritual battle, let us remember the promise in Romans 8:37-39, which assures us that nothing can separate us from the love of God in Christ Jesus our Lord. Whether we face tribulations, distress, or persecution, our victory is secured in Him. We are more than conquerors through Him who loved us.

In conclusion, while Satan is a persistent adversary, his power is limited compared to the sovereign might of God. With the armor of God securely in place, a robust prayer life, and the support of a faith-filled community, believers can navigate through life's trials and tribulations with confidence. Let us remain vigilant, grounded in the Word of God, and connected to our source of power—our Heavenly Father. This is how we overcome the world's darkness and maintain our light, shining brightly as beacons of hope and truth in a world that desperately needs the message of the gospel.

Result of succumbing to Satan's temptations to live beyond our means, spurred by envy and the desire for immediate gratification. This financial bondage not only stresses our material resources but also our spiritual well-being, as it shifts our focus from God's provisions to our shortages and desires.

Likewise, if pride is our weakness, Satan will exploit this to sow discord and division, encouraging us to view ourselves as superior to others, which can lead to isolation and conflict within our community and families. He knows that pride can make us resistant to the counsel and accountability that are crucial for spiritual growth and health.

In the area of relationships, Satan often stirs up old grievances and fosters unforgiveness to destroy bonds between family, friends, and church members. By keeping us entrenched in bitterness, he prevents the healing and unity that come through forgiving as we have been forgiven by Christ.

For those struggling with lust, Satan tempts with impurity in thoughts and actions, leading to sin that can devastate relationships and personal integrity. He bombards the mind with immoral images and opportunities, hoping to entrap his targets in a cycle of guilt and shame.

However, it is crucial to remember that Satan's power is not ultimate. God has provided us with the means to overcome every temptation and to stand firm against the devil's schemes. Ephesians 6:10-18 instructs us to put on the whole armor of God so that we can stand against the wiles of the devil. This includes girding ourselves with truth, wearing the breastplate of righteousness, and taking up the shield of faith to quench all the fiery darts of the wicked.

James 4:7-8 offers a promise and a command that is both simple and profound: "Submit yourselves therefore to God. Resist the devil, and he will flee from you. Draw nigh to God, and he will draw nigh to you." This scripture reminds us that closeness to God is our best defense against Satan. By living a life of prayer, rooted in the Scriptures, and surrounded by a supportive faith community, we ensure that Satan finds no foothold.

God's promise to His children is clear: He will never leave us nor forsake us (Hebrews 13:5). As we stay connected to Him, our weaknesses become areas of growth and testimony, demonstrating His power to save and sustain. We must constantly seek God's strength and wisdom to navigate the challenges posed by our spiritual adversary.

As we confront our personal weaknesses and rely on God's strength, we must also engage in proactive spiritual practices. Regular confession, accountability, and community support are critical. We must cultivate humility, recognizing our dependence on God's grace, and encourage one another to live in ways that honor Him.

In summary, while Satan is adept at identifying and attacking our weaknesses, our defense lies in our relationship with God, our adherence to His Word, and our connection with the body of Christ. Through these divine resources, we can overcome the enemy's strategies and live victorious lives, marked by spiritual health and freedom.

Is in this obedience and continual submission to God's Word that true peace and protection are found. As we invite God's presence into our lives and homes through prayer, worship, and the diligent study of His Word, we create an environment where the Holy Spirit can freely operate and where Satan's influence is weakened.

The promises of God become the framework through which we view life's challenges and trials. Even when Satan attempts to bring about discouragement and despair, the truth of God's Word counteracts his lies, reminding us of the victory that is already won in Christ. This knowledge empowers us to stand firm, resist the enemy's advances, and pursue righteousness.

Remember, Satan's tactics are designed to disrupt your spiritual equilibrium and distract you from God's purpose for your life. He aims to steal your joy, kill your faith, and destroy your relationships. However, the armor of God—comprising the belt of truth, the breastplate of righteousness, the shield of faith, the helmet of salvation, and the sword of the Spirit—is not only defensive but also offensive. It equips you to actively combat the lies and attacks of the enemy.

As you continue to walk in the light of God's truth, keep in mind that each step you take in obedience is a step towards greater spiritual maturity and deeper fellowship with God. This journey is not without its obstacles, but the Holy Spirit is your guide and comforter, leading you through every challenge and equipping you to overcome.

Stay vigilant against the subtle whispers of doubt that Satan may plant in your mind. Be proactive in renewing your mind daily with the truths found in Scripture (Romans 12:2). By doing so, you maintain a strong defense against the enemy's deceptions and build a resilient faith that is not easily shaken.

In your spiritual walk, cultivate an atmosphere of worship and gratitude. This attitude aligns your heart with God's, fortifies your spirit against spiritual warfare, and opens the door to God's abundant blessings and peace. As you praise and worship God, you affirm His sovereignty over your life and acknowledge His place as the ultimate authority.

Through these practices, not only will you find personal peace and spiritual growth, but you will also set an example for others in your home and community. Your steadfastness in the faith can inspire others to seek God and to put on their own spiritual armor.

God is always working in the lives of those who love Him and are called according to His purpose (Romans 8:28). Trust that He is orchestrating everything for your good and His glory, even when the path seems fraught with difficulties. With God on your side, no strategy of Satan can prevail against you. As you walk in obedience and faith, you will experience the fullness of life that God intends for you, characterized by His peace, protection, and presence.

My medical diagnosis of Parkinson's Disease in 2018 was a devastating blow to my family and I. God was the only source of strength to help us understand the impact this disease will have on our family. I was shaken by the new reality of what new adjustments that would have to be made to accommodate a different way of doing things.

Prayer and worship in our home became more essential to understand what God was up to. And so we quickly began to see God's sovereign will and plan shaping my family's future through the hills and valleys of life and what that meant to my family.

When our trust in God began to waver because we did not see the whole picture of His workings in our home, my family to slowly began to drift from the presence of God to living careless lives. Our view of God was that He is not doing the things He said He would do for us. Lots of negative thoughts began to flood into the minds of everyone in my home.

And thus, in a moment when were slack in our vigilance and watchfulness over our lives, the enemy was lurking for the opportunity to come in to plant the seed of doubt that would have the family questions God's faithfulness to our family and the promises He made to us. Satan saw the right opportunity to do his mischief. And so our family made a commitment to read, study, and meditate on God's word every single day.

God continues to be our only source of strength and comfort. Despite the physical challenges associated with Parkinson's disease and the relentless spiritual warfare, His presence provided a sense of peace and resilience. Even when I doubted, His mercy remained steadfast, demonstrating that His love is not contingent on our perfection but on His boundless grace and His infinite mercy.

The journey with Parkinson's disease has been arduous, but it has also been a profound testament to the power of faith and the importance of community and family support. The trials I have faced have not only tested my physical and spiritual resilience but have deepened my reliance on God's promises and His provision.

My family's unwavering support, coupled with God's grace, has helped me navigate the complexities and the pains associated with this disease. I am convinced that God allowed this affliction int my life because of what I now see where my life was heading at the speed I was going, heading in the wrong direction.

Through it all, my understanding of God's character has grown. I have learned that He is not a punisher of our missteps but a redeemer of our souls. He uses our trials not to break us but to build us into stronger, more compassionate individuals. This ordeal has taught me the invaluable lesson that our weaknesses are opportunities for God to display His strength and mercy. In my weakest moments, when I felt utterly powerless, God's spirit was a comforting and empowering presence, reassuring me that I am never alone.

Reflecting on this journey, I realize that every prayer, every tear, and every moment of despair was enveloped in God's loving response. He never left my side, even when I was overwhelmed by fear and pain. The notion that God was punishing me was a deception from the enemy, aimed at sapping my hope and diminishing my faith. However, the truth of God's word and His promises became the anchor during those tumultuous times.

God's faithfulness extends beyond our human understanding. He is with us in the darkest valleys and the highest mountains. The challenges I faced were not just physical but spiritual battles, where the enemy sought to take advantage of my vulnerability. Yet, God equipped me and my family with the strength to withstand and overcome these attacks. His words were our defense, a reminder that we are more than conquerors through Him who loved us (Romans 8:37).

As I continue to live with Parkinson's Disease, my faith is my fortress. Despite the physical limitations, my spirit remains invigorated by God's assurances. My home, filled with His presence, is a sanctuary where fear and uncertainty are replaced by peace and certainty in God's care.

To anyone struggling with health issues or spiritual doubts, remember that God's love is unchanging. He is not the author of our pain but our healer and sustainer. Lean into His eternal promises, and let His truth fortify your heart against any fear or despair. God's plans for us are always for our good, to give us a future and a hope (Jeremiah 29:11). Embrace His presence, and let it transform your trials into testimonies of His enduring faithfulness and love. Without a test there is no testimony.

See the good side of every negative situation and the bright side of any dark moment. God will work all things, whether good or bad, for the good of everyone who loves Him. They are the ones He has called to His purpose (Romans 8:28). Nothing is hard for the Lord God to do for humanity. Many times, it is our perspective that affects how we see life. The Bible says that the darkness and light are alike to God (Psalms 139;12). So it does matter what your situation or circumstance is, God has the solution to your problem and an answer to your question.

Remember, you are now living in the freedom Christ offers—not just a temporary reprieve from troubles but a profound transformation of life. As Romans 6:4 states, "We were therefore buried with him through baptism into death in order that, just as Christ was raised from the dead through the glory of the Father, we too may live a new life." This new life in Christ is about more than escaping the old; it's about embracing an entirely new way of being that aligns with God's divine purposes and leads us towards eternal life.

It is crucial for every believer to steadfastly hold onto their faith, especially when confronted with the trials and tribulations that life invariably throws our way. These challenges, while daunting, are not insurmountable with God by our side. They are opportunities for growth, meant to strengthen our faith and deepen our reliance on Him. As James 1:2-4 encourages, "Consider it pure joy, my brothers and sisters, whenever you face trials of many kinds, because you know that the testing of your faith produces perseverance. Let perseverance finish its work so that you may be mature and complete, not lacking anything."

In your journey with Christ, be vigilant and mindful of the adversary's schemes to derail your faith through fear, doubt, and temptation. The enemy prides himself on exploiting our weaknesses, but our strength lies in Christ, who has already overcome the world. By remaining anchored in the Word of God and steadfast in prayer, you fortify yourself against these assaults. Ephesians 6:13-18 outlines the full armor of God which every believer must wear to stand firm against the tactics of the devil.

Embrace the community of believers God has placed in your life, just as the members of your church have supported you through prayer and fellowship. This community is invaluable, not only for the comfort and encouragement it provides but also as a source of accountability and spiritual strength. Hebrews 10:24-25 reminds us, "And let us consider how we may spur one another on toward love and good deeds, not giving up meeting together, as some are in the habit of doing, but encouraging one another—and all the more as you see the Day approaching."

Finally, never underestimate the power of sharing your testimony. Just as you have been moved and supported by others, your story can inspire and uplift those around you. Your experiences and the lessons you've learned can help others facing similar struggles, providing them with hope and a pathway to healing. In sharing your journey, you not only bear witness to God's faithfulness but also perpetuate a cycle of blessing, strengthening the faith of others and expanding the reach of God's kingdom.

As you continue to navigate your challenges, remember that God's promises are sure and His love is unfailing. He will never leave you nor forsake you (Deuteronomy 31:6). Continue to trust in His word, lean on His strength, and walk in the light of His truth. Your path may be difficult, but with God, all things are possible (Matthew 19:26). Keep your eyes fixed on Jesus, the author and perfecter of our faith (Hebrews 12:2), and let His peace rule in your hearts, knowing that in Him, you are more than conquerors (Romans 8:37).

So, understand the urgency of this decision. The call to embrace the gospel of Jesus Christ is not just an invitation—it is an urgent command to come out of darkness into His marvelous light. It is an opportunity to escape from the impending judgment and to secure a place in eternity with God, where there is no sorrow, no pain, and no death.

This decision is not to be taken lightly or postponed. Every moment counts, and the decision you make today about Jesus Christ could affect your eternity. In Hebrews 3:15, it says, "Today, if you hear his voice, do not harden your hearts as you did in the rebellion." This verse emphasizes the immediacy and the seriousness of responding to God's call.

Do not be deceived by the transient pleasures of this world or by the lies that Satan might whisper in your ear, suggesting that you have plenty of time to decide or that you can make it on your own without God's grace. Such thoughts are designed to lead you astray, to keep you bound in sin, and ultimately to destroy you.

Instead, recognize the incredible love of God, who sent His only Son to die on the cross so that through His sacrifice, you might be saved from sin and its eternal consequences. John 3:16 clearly states, "For God so loved the world that he gave his one and only Son, that whoever believes in him shall not perish but have eternal life." This is the core of the gospel—the good news that salvation is available to all who will believe in Jesus Christ.

Accepting Jesus as your Savior means acknowledging your need for Him, repenting of your sins, and trusting in His finished work on the cross. It means turning away from a life led by sin and instead, following Him in a new life guided by His Spirit.

The journey of faith is not without its challenges, but it is the only path that leads to true and lasting peace. By surrendering your life to Christ, you are not giving up your freedom; rather, you are stepping into the true freedom that only He can provide—a freedom from guilt, shame, and the eternal consequences of sin.

As you contemplate this decision, remember that God is not distant or uninterested in your struggles. He is close, He hears your doubts and fears, and He is waiting for you to call upon Him. He is ready to show you great and mighty things which you do not know (Jeremiah 33:3).

If you feel the Holy Spirit moving in your heart today, do not resist. Open your heart to the transformative power of the gospel. Commit to living according to God's ways and witness how He can change not only your life but also the lives of those around you.

Make the decision to follow Jesus today. It is the most important decision you will ever make, with eternal implications. Pray to God, asking Him to give you the courage to step out in faith, to leave behind the old life of sin, and to begin a new life in Christ. Remember, there is no better time than now, and no assurance of a tomorrow. Embrace the gift of salvation and start your journey toward a fulfilling and everlasting life with God.

This reason that He sent His Son, Jesus Christ, to provide a way back to Himself—a way that leads through repentance and faith. Jesus's sacrifice on the cross was not merely a historical event; it was the definitive action that opened the door for reconciliation between God and man. Through Christ, we are not only saved from sin but given a new identity and a new purpose.

As we face the fleeting nature of our earthly lives, it becomes imperative to understand the urgency and importance of the gospel. Life is indeed like a vapor, appearing for a little while and then vanishing, as James 4:14 describes. This stark reality should drive us to consider our spiritual state and the eternal implications of our choices. Every moment is an opportunity to align ourselves with God's will, to embrace the life He offers, and to fulfill the purpose for which we were created.

In a world fraught with uncertainty, where tomorrow is not promised, the decision to follow Jesus is the most crucial one we can make. Postponing this decision can lead to eternal consequences. The Bible warns us repeatedly of the brevity of life and the urgency to secure our eternal destiny through Christ. Hebrews 9:27 states, "Just as people are destined to die once, and after that to face judgment." This verse underscores the inevitability of death and the inescapable reality of judgment that follows.

Therefore, it is not enough to merely acknowledge the existence of God or to appreciate the moral teachings of Jesus. Salvation requires a commitment, a turning away from sin, and a turning toward Christ with faith and obedience. It requires recognizing Jesus as Lord and Savior, and submitting to His lordship in every area of life.

For those who have yet to make this decision, the message is clear: do not delay. The deception of thinking there is always more time can be fatal. Satan, the deceiver and enemy of our souls, seeks to lull humanity into a false sense of security, encouraging procrastination on spiritual matters. His tactics may include distracting us with the cares of this life, the pursuit of wealth, pleasure, or even the fear of what others may think if we choose to follow Christ.

Conversely, God's call is to wake up from spiritual lethargy and recognize the signs of the times, to see the reality of our spiritual condition, and to understand the critical importance of now. 2 Corinthians 6:2 tells us, "For he says, 'In the time of my favor I heard you, and in the day of salvation I helped you.' I tell you, now is the time of God's favor, now is the day of salvation."

The true church of God must stand as a beacon of truth in a world that increasingly embraces deception. Believers are called to not only uphold the truth of the gospel but to actively share it, fighting the good fight of faith and contending earnestly for the faith once delivered to the saints (Jude 1:3). As followers of Christ, we are equipped with the Holy Spirit, empowered to overcome the lies of the enemy, and driven by the love of God to reach out to those who are still walking in darkness.

In conclusion, remember that our time here is short, and we must use it wisely, not as an excuse for fear, but as motivation to live fully for God, fulfilling His purpose for our lives. Let us then approach each day with urgency, passion, and dedication to the gospel, knowing that through Jesus Christ, we have the hope of eternity and the promise of His return. Let us hold fast to our confession of faith without wavering, for He who promised is faithful (Hebrews 10:23).

Navigating through such tumultuous environments requires vigilance, discernment, and a steadfast commitment to the principles taught by Jesus Christ. As believers, it is crucial to stay grounded in the Scriptures, constantly seeking the guidance of the Holy Spirit to discern the genuine from the counterfeit, the truth from deception. This is especially important in congregations where, as Jesus described, tares might grow alongside the wheat. It is these tares—those influences or individuals that mimic the truth but ultimately serve to disrupt and destroy—that pose a significant threat to the unity and purity of the church.

The Apostle Paul urges believers in Ephesians 4:14-15 to "no longer be children, tossed to and fro by the waves and carried about by every wind of doctrine, by human cunning, by craftiness in deceitful schemes. Rather, speaking the truth in love, we are to grow up in every way into him who is the head, into Christ." This maturity in faith enables Christians to recognize and resist the subtle tactics of the enemy.

For those in leadership positions within the church, there is a greater responsibility to uphold and model godliness. James 3:1 warns, "Not many of you should become teachers, my brothers, for you know that we who teach will be judged with greater strictness." This admonition serves as a reminder that the role of guiding others spiritually is not to be taken lightly. Leaders are accountable not only for their actions but also for the spiritual well-being of those they lead.

Marriage, as a sacred institution, also calls for careful consideration and divine guidance. The decision to marry should be made with prayerful discernment and a clear understanding of God's will. As 2 Corinthians 6:14 advises, "Do not be unequally yoked with unbelievers. For what partnership has righteousness with lawlessness? Or what fellowship has light with darkness?" This principle is not just about avoiding potential conflicts; it is about fostering a relationship that glorifies God and reflects His love and commitment.

It is equally important for individual believers to remain alert to the spiritual condition of their own hearts. The parable of the sower, as found in Matthew 13, illustrates how the seed of the Word can fall on different types of soil—a metaphor for the state of our hearts. Those choked by "the cares of this world and the deceitfulness of riches" are unable to bear fruit. Believers must therefore cultivate a heart that is receptive to God's Word, allowing it to take root and produce a harvest of righteousness.

In confronting the challenges within and outside the church, the armor of God (Ephesians 6:10-18) provides the necessary spiritual protection. This armor includes truth, righteousness, the gospel of peace, faith, salvation, and the Word of God, which is the sword of the Spirit. Armed with these, believers can stand firm against the schemes of the devil, ensuring that their faith remains intact and their witness unblemished.

Ultimately, the church must strive to maintain its purity and commitment to the gospel, recognizing that it is not immune to the influences of the world. The call to holiness is a collective and individual responsibility. Each member must contribute to the health and vitality of the body of Christ by living a life that is true to the teachings of Jesus and by actively engaging in practices that foster spiritual growth and unity.

As the world grows increasingly complex and as challenges within and outside the church continue to arise, the message of the gospel must remain clear and undiluted. Believers are called to be light in the darkness, salt in a world that is losing its flavor, and a beacon of truth in an age of deception. By standing firm in faith and committed to the truth, the church can not only withstand the attacks of the enemy but also thrive, drawing many into the saving knowledge of Jesus Christ.

This stark warning serves as a critical reminder for every believer to be vigilant and committed to the path of righteousness. The imagery used in Revelation to describe the downfall of Babylon and the dire consequences of allegiance to the Beast underscores the severity of turning away from God. It illustrates the spiritual battle that rages over the souls of humanity, where the stakes are eternal life or eternal damnation.

As Christians, we are called to be discerning, to test every spirit, and to hold fast to the teachings of Scripture. 1 John 4:1 advises, "Beloved, do not believe every spirit, but test the spirits to see whether they are from God, for many false prophets have gone out into the world." This command is crucial in a world where the lines between truth and error can often appear blurred. It's essential for believers to rely on the Holy Spirit for guidance and to immerse themselves in God's Word to recognize the deceit that may otherwise lead them astray.

Furthermore, the call to "Come out of her, my people," from Revelation 18:4, is a divine directive to separate ourselves from the corrupt systems of this world that contradict God's ways. This separation is not just physical but profoundly spiritual. It involves renouncing all practices, systems, and values that are inherently sinful and contrary to God's holy nature. This is particularly challenging in today's culture, where moral relativism and materialism pervade, tempting believers to conform to worldly standards rather than God's commandments.

The resistance to this call often comes from a place of fear—fear of loss, fear of rejection, or fear of persecution. However, Scripture repeatedly encourages believers to stand firm. For example, Joshua 1:9 commands, "Have I not commanded you? Be strong and courageous. Do not be frightened, and do not be dismayed, for the Lord your God is with you wherever you go." This assurance is the bedrock upon which believers can stand when facing the pressures and temptations of this world.

The narrative of Babylon and the Beast also serves as a sobering reminder of the reality of God's judgment. Those who choose to align with the corrupt systems of this world and worship the Beast will face the full wrath of God, as detailed vividly in Revelation. This should motivate every believer not only to live a life pleasing to God but also to engage in evangelism—to reach out to those who are still lost, sharing the truth of the gospel and the love of Christ that can save them from impending judgment.

In confronting the end times and the rise of apostasy, believers must remember that they are not powerless. Armed with the truth of the gospel and empowered by the Holy Spirit, they can overcome the deceptions of the enemy. Ephesians 6:11-12 reminds us to "Put on the whole armor of God, that you may be able to stand against the schemes of the devil. For we do not wrestle against flesh and blood, but against the rulers, against the authorities, against the cosmic powers over this present darkness, against the spiritual forces of evil in the heavenly places."

Ultimately, the call to come out of Babylon is a call to holiness, to unwavering faith, and to a commitment to the Kingdom of God that transcends earthly allegiances. It is a call to prioritize eternal values over temporal gain, to seek first the Kingdom of God and His righteousness (Matthew 6:33). As believers, our mission is to live out this call daily, demonstrating through our lives the transforming power of the gospel and the hope that we have in Christ. This mission is not just for our benefit but for the salvation of many who are still caught in the deception of the enemy, providing a beacon of light in an increasingly dark world.

In light of the serious spiritual warfare described, it's crucial for believers to actively seek wisdom and discernment from God to navigate through the lies and deception that saturate our world. The adversary, Satan, is cunning and relentless, employing every tool at his disposal to lead people away from the truth of the gospel. It's not just about resisting overt evil; it's also about recognizing the subtler forms of deception that can seep into our lives and our communities.

Discernment and Vigilance

The need for discernment cannot be overstated. 1 John 4:1-3 provides a clear directive to test every spirit to determine whether it is from God. This involves more than just a surface check; it requires a deep understanding of Scripture and a close relationship with God through prayer and fellowship with other believers. This testing is crucial because false prophets and teachers often appear genuine, perhaps even charismatic, but their message is contrary to the teachings of Christ.

The Role of Community

As members of the body of Christ, we are not meant to face these challenges alone. Fellowship with other believers provides strength and accountability. It helps us to grow in our faith and to stand firm against the schemes of the devil. Moreover, the community serves as a check against deception, as we can help one another discern truth from falsehood through collective wisdom and scriptural grounding.

Practical Steps to Guard Against Deception

Regular Study of Scripture: Immerse yourself in the Bible daily. Understanding God's Word is the best defense against the enemy's lies.

Prayer: Engage in constant prayer, asking God for wisdom, strength, and discernment. Pray not just for yourself but also for your community and for those who may be deceived.

Fellowship: Actively participate in church and small group activities where you can build relationships and grow with others who are committed to living according to God's Word.

Worship: Regular worship refocuses our minds on God and His truth, counteracting the world's noise and the enemy's lies.

Outreach and Evangelism: Share the gospel. The act of speaking truth not only helps others but also reinforces our own faith and understanding of God's Word.

Avoiding the Snares of the Enemy

Beware of modern-day idolatry, which can be subtler than ancient forms. Today, idolatry can involve excessive reliance on technology, obsession with social media, or even the idolization of celebrities and public figures. These distractions can lead us away from God and make us susceptible to the deceptions of the enemy.

Additionally, be cautious of the spiritual and moral relativism that pervades our culture. This worldview rejects absolute truth, which is a direct contradiction to the teachings of Scripture. Standing firm in God's absolute truths is essential in a world that increasingly values personal truth over universal truth.

Conclusion

As you navigate through your spiritual journey, remember that the battle is not just against flesh and blood but against spiritual forces of evil (Ephesians 6:12). Equipping yourself with the full armor of God (Ephesians 6:13-18) is essential for standing firm against these forces.

Living a life of vigilance and dedication to Christ is not about fear, but about freedom—the freedom to live a life of purpose, integrity, and joy in the Lord. By staying rooted in God's Word, engaged in prayer, connected with the community of believers, and vigilant against the enemy's schemes, you can ensure that your path is aligned with God's will, leading to a fulfilling and fruitful life in Christ.

This powerful reminder from Scripture underscores the crucial importance of obedience to God and the dangers of deviating from His commandments. The story of Saul seeking counsel from a medium, as detailed in 1 Samuel 28, serves as a stern warning against turning to forbidden sources for guidance and the inevitable spiritual downfall that follows such decisions.

The Consequences of Disobedience

Saul's descent into spiritual darkness began with disobedience. His failure to fully obey God's commands led to a gradual but significant separation from God, culminating in his tragic decision to seek counsel from a source that God had explicitly condemned. This act of desperation not only violated God's law but also highlighted Saul's complete estrangement from the Lord, who had stopped communicating with him due to his persistent disobedience.

The Danger of Seeking Forbidden Knowledge

The appeal to forbidden sources of knowledge, such as mediums, psychics, or any form of witchcraft, is a common pitfall for those who have strayed from God's path. These sources can seem appealing in desperate times, offering quick answers and insights, but they are fraught with spiritual dangers. The information they provide, even if it appears accurate or mimics truth, is sourced from deception and lies, orchestrated by Satan to lead further away from God.

The Nature of Satanic Deception

Satan is skilled in deception, using half-truths and twisted facts to lure individuals into sin. The encounter Saul had with the spirit impersonating Samuel is a prime example of such deception. While the spirit recounted events accurately enough to convince Saul, its presence was a direct result of Saul's disobedience and desperation, not a legitimate channel of divine communication. This event emphasizes that Satan and his agents can manipulate known facts to create convincing lies.

Staying Anchored in God's Word

To avoid the pitfalls of deception and disobedience, believers must stay firmly anchored in God's Word. Scripture is the ultimate standard against which all teachings and spiritual experiences must be measured. If any spiritual guidance or revelation contradicts the Bible, it is not from God.

Living in Obedience and the Power of the Holy Spiri-

Believers have the indwelling Holy Spirit, who guides and teaches in accordance with God's Word. The Holy Spirit will never lead a believer into sin or contradict what God has revealed in the Scriptures. Instead, He convicts of sin, guides in truth, and empowers believers to live lives pleasing to God.

Sin and Its Universal Consequence

The narrative of mankind's fall into sin as recorded in Genesis underscores the universal nature of sin and its consequences. Every human inherits this sinful nature, which is the root cause to disobedience and rebellion against God's commands. However, through Christ's redemptive work on the cross, non-believers are transformed into believers who are given a new nature and the power to overcome Satan's temptations.

Repentance and Restoration

For those who find themselves caught in a life of disobedience or have strayed from God's path, the call to repentance is always open but this open door of God's mercy, grace, love, forgiveness, and compassion for sinners will not last forever. God's desire is not to condemn but to restore. He wants to restore to Himself through the finished work of Jesus Christ on the cross at Calvery, all mankind to a life of holiness and purity in the presence of God.

It is Christ who paid the enormous debt with His body in which He bore the sins of the world when it is humanity who should have paid the debt, they owe what the law of God demanded. As 1 John 1:9 assures, "If we confess our sins, he is faithful and just to forgive us our sins and to cleanse us from all unrighteousness." Thus, the redeemed children of God are set free from the bondage to sin. The promise that God had made to mankind, that if they would diligently seek Him out in His Word with all their mind, heart, and soul they will find Him (Deuteronomy 4:29 and Hebrews 5:6). It is Jesus Christ who holds the key to breaking mankind free from the cycle of sin and rebellion and restoring them to a place to have fellowship with God.

Conclusion

The life of a believer is one of continual growth and vigilance against the schemes of the enemy. By remaining rooted in Scripture, guided by the Holy Spirit, and committed to obedience, believers can safeguard themselves against the deceptions and temptations that lead to spiritual ruin. Let the story of Saul serve as a reminder of the dire consequences of forsaking God's commandments and the unchanging truth that God's ways are always best.

Husbands and Fathers, our Home Is our Responsibility.

The narrative of Adam and Eve's fall into sin, as depicted in Genesis, provides profound insights into the nature of temptation, the consequences of disobedience, and the roles and responsibilities within a marriage as intended by God. This story illustrates not only the subtlety of Satan's deceptions but also highlights the profound impact of our responses to such temptations.

The Subtlety of Satan's Temptations

Satan's approach to Eve was cunning, exploiting her innocence to sin and temptation. Adam and Eve have never been in an environment where the truth of God's Word (commands) would come into question by a lying being, Satan, disguised in a created creature of God, a serpent. This animal was chosen by Satan for its subtlety and its appearance of being non-threatening. Satan used his deceptive devices to trap Eve by using logic they were not created with to reason with him in questioning the truthfulness and reliability of God and His Word. God spoke His command clearly for

Adam and Eve to hear and understand. By questioning God's command and suggesting that God was withholding something good from her, Satan planted seeds of doubt in Eve's mind. This tactic is still employed by Satan today to tempt individuals away from obedience to God. He often present sin as something desirable or beneficial, masking its destructive nature.

The Role of Mutual Accountability in Marriage

Adam's passive role during the encounter illustrates a failure in spiritual leadership and protection in their relationship. As partners, both Adam and Eve were responsible for supporting and upholding one another in obedience to God. This mutual accountability is crucial in all Christian relationships but especially in marriage, where spouses are called to encourage and protect each other's spiritual well-being.

Spiritual Adultery

The concept of spiritual adultery, as was highlighted earlier, extends beyond physical unfaithfulness to include any form of unfaithfulness to God. Engaging with sinful practices, nurturing sinful thoughts, or forming allegiances that lead us away from God can all be forms of spiritual adultery. For believers, being "married" to Christ means that our loyalty and devotion should be to Him above all else. Any relationship or engagement that draws us away from that commitment can be seen as an act of infidelity against our spiritual union with Christ.

The Importance of Spiritual Vigilance

Adam and Eve's story is a stark reminder of the need for spiritual vigilance. Just as they were instructed to guard and keep the garden, Christians are called to guard their hearts and minds, being mindful of the influences they allow into their lives. Proverbs 4:23 advises, "Above all else, guard your heart, for everything you do flows from it." This involves regular self-examination, prayer, and immersion in Scripture to ensure that one's life aligns with God's will.

Lessons and Application

Awareness of Spiritual Warfare: Christians must be aware that they are in a constant battle against spiritual forces seeking to lead them astray. Recognizing the strategies of the enemy is the first step in countering them.

The Power of God's Word: Just as Jesus used Scripture to counter Satan's temptations (Matthew 4:1-11), believers should also use the truth of God's Word to refute lies and resist temptations.

The Need for Community Support: The church community plays a vital role in supporting individuals in their spiritual journey. Believers can draw strength and encouragement from fellow Christians, which helps in maintaining spiritual health and accountability.

Continuous Growth in Faith: Adding to one's faith with virtues such as knowledge, temperance, patience, godliness, brotherly kindness, and love, as mentioned in 2 Peter 1, strengthens one's spiritual foundation, making it difficult for Satan to find a foothold.

Living a life that is pleasing to God involves a continuous commitment to holiness and a conscious effort to avoid situations that might lead to sin.

In conclusion, the fall of Adam and Eve is not just an account of the origin of sin but also a lesson-packed story for all believers. It calls for vigilance, spiritual maturity, and a committed heart towards God. Understanding and applying these principles helps believers not only to avoid the pitfalls that led to the fall but also to grow stronger in their relationship with God and each other.

Adam erred, in that he may have neglected his responsibility to be the constant covering presence of the wife he wanted and did receive from his Creator. Adam was God's representative in the home of the Adams. Husbands, we are to take heed of our role and our position in our homes. We are to be Christ's representative in our homes, and thus, the spiritual covering of our families.

Husbands must always protect their families from the attacks of the enemy by being God-fearing and obedient to the commands of Christ. Satan is only able to destroy many families, mainly because the husband is usually the one who is in rebellion against God.

Many husbands are to be blamed for the spiritual dryness and deadness in their homes. Some husbands present a form of godliness but deny the power of God to fully operate in their lives and in their homes. One can only conclude that the reason some Christian homes are less Christlike and are becoming more world-like is there is at least one member in the home that is in rebellion against God, and sometimes that person is the husband and father.

When we are asleep spiritually, it affects our fellowship with God. Everyone in the home is affected by the sin or the sins of the one who has trespassed against God. Genuine Christ-centered family worship is absolutely necessary to keep us connected to God and to guard our homes against Satan's attacks. If the husband is, at least, the one wearing the armor of God in his home and if he is sober and vigilant in the Word of God so that his living is right before Him, God is able to use him as the flaming swords to keep his home from the hands of Satan and use him as an instrument of righteousness to destroy the works of wickedness that may be in his home.

It has been my experience that some of us church leaders are not being the physical and spiritual leaders in our homes, the way God has defined our roles to be, in His Word. We are not just "the man of the house," as some of us like to say and think of ourselves to be such. We represent God to our families. And they ought to see Christ in us and see Him in everything that we do.

And God ought to see Himself in our living. We are not going to be perfect human beings as long as we live in this world and we have a carnal nature to deal with. But that does not mean that you and I should not strive to be perfect as our Heavenly Father is perfect. He is to be our object teacher. We must look to God to be the kind of fathers and husbands that he wants us to be.

We may not get it right the first or the second time. We are still going to make mistakes because we are growing in Christ, and we are the Master's work in progress. But at least we are on the road where God wants us to be, and He will pick us up if we fall and will gently guide us along the way to becoming better husbands and fathers.

And so fathers and husbands are not to be dry and miserable and be the unwilling providers for our families. Christ is our object lesson. He gave Himself for us, where He provided all that we will ever need. And that which we are not, He will be that and so much more to us.

As a society, we have this thing wrong. Fatherhood and husband-hood are not just to be the breadwinner if that is what we think we are only supposed to be. We have to provide emotional, psychological, sociological, and spiritual and leadership support for ourselves and our families. We are to get these principles from the Word of God, irrespective of how our fathers raised or did not raise us.

should be coachable, learnable, approachable, and teachable so that we can glean the gems of godly and victorious living from the Word of God. God is our Father, and He loves and cares for us more than our earthly father cared for us. In many cases, some of them might have done their best to be the best husband and father in their home. But we must break the cycle of dysfunctionality to move on to higher heights with God. And so Satan is not our father. God is our Father, who is in heaven. Hallowed be His name.

Some of us have made leadership all about the flock of God in the church and not about the flock of God in the home. But weak and ineffective home leaders make poor and ineffective leaders in the church. If we cannot take care of the work of governing our home with godly fear, which God has given us to manage efficiently, how are we going to do the work of God in the church? He is going to hold us accountable regarding our stewardship over our home.

Your reflection on the responsibilities of husbands and fathers within the Christian home highlights crucial Biblical teachings and brings to the fore the spiritual and familial duties ordained by God. The role of a husband and father, as described, is foundational in shaping a godly family, underscoring the need for a Christ-centered approach to family life.

Spiritual Leadership in the Home

As husbands and fathers, the responsibility to lead spiritually does not merely rest on conducting family worship or prayers but permeates every aspect of home life. This leadership involves teaching, correcting, and guiding the family according to God's Word. Ephesians 5:25-28 eloquently instructs husbands to love their wives as Christ loved the church, sacrificing Himself for her sanctification. This sacrificial love is the model for husbands, encompassing spiritual nurturing and protective care.

The Challenge of Worldly Influences

In today's society, where secular values often contradict Biblical principles, the role of a Christian father becomes even more pivotal. The pressure from contemporary culture can dilute the spiritual focus and integrity of a family. As you noted, it is imperative that fathers shield their children not just from physical harm but more significantly from spiritual and moral decay. Proverbs 22:6 isn't just a directive; it's a strategic approach to ensure that children grow up with a solid understanding of truth and faith, which helps them navigate life's complexities.

Dealing with Spiritual Lethargy

The increasing rates of divorce and decline in family worship within Christian homes are alarming but reflect the broader spiritual battles against the family unit. Addressing these issues requires more than discipline; it demands a revival of genuine faith and commitment within the home. Spiritual lethargy can creep into any household, and combating this inertia starts with the spiritual vitality of the father himself.

Continuous Spiritual Engagement

The call to be continuously engaged in spiritual activities such as prayer, worship, and Bible study is not just about maintaining religious routines but about fostering a living relationship with God that each family member can witness and emulate. It's about creating a home where the presence of God is tangible, influencing all interactions and decisions.

Intercessory Role

Your emphasis on the intercessory role of the husband is particularly poignant. Just as Christ intercedes for His church, so must husbands intercede for their families. This intercession is a profound duty that involves praying against the spiritual decay mirrored in rebellion or disobedience within the family. It's about seeking divine intervention and transformation for the hearts and minds of family members.

Provision and Dependence on God

Lastly, the dual role of spiritual and physical provider is critical. Relying on God for provision does not negate a father's effort; instead, it enhances his capacity to provide through divine guidance and wisdom. It recognizes God as the ultimate source while employing one's abilities and opportunities to their fullest potential under God's direction.

In summary, the Biblical blueprint for husbands and fathers is comprehensive, intertwining spiritual, emotional, and physical provisions, all rooted in a deep, transformative relationship with God. This design ensures that when fathers align with God's will and teachings, they can effectively counter the cultural tides, lead their families with wisdom and courage, and foster homes that honor God in all aspects. This high calling is neither simple nor easy, but with God's grace, it is the path to profound spiritual fulfillment and family unity.

17 Glenn T. Stanton, Focus on the Family, published February 2011.

There are numerous examples throughout the Bible of generational rebellion, as seen in the lives of its most notable figures. Cain, the son of Adam, defied God's commandments on the proper way to honor Him through worship and offerings. Disobedience to God's commandments is a sin that exposes us to severe consequences.

Interestingly, the curse of disobedience, which began with Adam's rebellion, was inherited by his son Cain, perpetuating the cycle of sin through all humanity. Romans 5:12 states, "Wherefore, as by one man sin entered the world, and death by sin; and so death passed on to all men, for that all have sinned." God's promises are unwavering—what one sows, one will reap, either reaping the rewards of obedience or suffering the consequences of disobedience.

Generational curses have plagued many families, including my own. If the seeds of rebellion and disobedience are not surrendered to God for destruction, they will continue to affect future generations. The responsibility falls on us—husbands and fathers, with God's assistance—to eradicate sin from our households. As designated high priests of our homes, we must diligently worship God and adhere to His word to prevent these curses from hindering our families' spiritual growth. Pride and ego can disconnect us from God's power and authority in our lives, potentially allowing Satan's influence to destroy everything within our homes. Only God can lead our families to victory over sin.

Therefore, as husbands and fathers, we are called by God to reflect the image of Christ, serving as high priests in our homes, and to fulfill our responsibilities with the love of Christ as our guide.

Satan's Limited Power

The devil does not possess absolute power; he only has as much power as God permits. He can influence our lives only if we allow him access. A small opening is all he needs to sow destruction. However, as long as we, the children of God, empowered by the Holy Spirit, adhere to God's commandments and follow Christ, Satan can gain no advantage over us.

If you are facing tribulations, it's because God has allowed these challenges to strengthen your faith and purify you. Despite appearances, your life isn't falling apart; instead, it's falling into place. God will guide you through these trials. Remember the story of Israel in Egypt; their deliverance came after more than four centuries of bondage. If you have resisted God's call to salvation, the turmoil in your life will persist until you surrender to His transformative power.

God allows Satan to test Christians to eliminate impurities from their lives, similar to Job's trials, where God permitted Satan to test him (Job 1:12). However, any affliction allowed by God is temporary and serves to strengthen our faith in Jesus Christ. Satan cannot freely afflict God's faithful without divine permission.

When our walk with God weakens, we become susceptible to Satan's temptations. Removing any part of the armor of God, even partially, can expose us to danger. As Proverbs warns, "Can a man scoop fire into his lap without his clothes being burned?"

Today, many churches are confronting serious challenges. Some have even welcomed individuals practicing lifestyles deemed sinful by traditional scriptural interpretations, including homosexuality, into leadership roles, asserting they are anointed by God to preach the Gospel. This controversial acceptance will be discussed further later on. Scripture warns that persistent sinfulness, unrepented, leads to destruction in the lake of fire. Those who subscribe to such lifestyles, refusing to repent, have succumbed to Satan's deception, believing doctrines that stray from biblical teachings. A true child of God must distance themselves from environments rife with false teachings.

However, all is not lost. Today still offers the promise of salvation through Jesus Christ, who died and shed His blood on the cross at Calvary. This sacrifice was made so that we might have life now and forever in paradise. God does not desire for anyone to perish but has created each of us for a purpose: to glorify Him and enjoy His blessings. Today, there is an opportunity to confess and repent of your sins to Jesus, receive forgiveness, and accept the gift of eternal life.

Many have already experienced the transformative power of the Holy Spirit, awakening them from spiritual death to rebirth in Christ. The decision you face is urgent and must be made now—before it's too late, before death or Christ's return. God is reaching out to you to escape the grip of Satan. He will not save those who remain in sin, and lifestyles contrary to His word, including unrepented homosexuality, are considered sinful. God's salvation involves rescuing sinners from sinful practices, not merely in thought but also in deed.

In some churches today, what should be sanctuaries of holiness have become stages for abominable acts. Individuals who profess Christianity yet engage in gross immorality are revealing their true allegiance—not to God, but to darkness. Practices like witchcraft and overt debauchery are performed openly, without shame. These individuals, referred to in scripture as "tares," will be separated from the "wheat" during divine judgment. The Bible warns that a great sifting within Christendom will occur, testing every deed to determine if it stems from righteousness or unrighteousness. This judgment is described as starting in the House of God (1 Peter 4:17), with an angel executing God's command to cleanse the church, as depicted in Revelation 14:19: "And the angel thrust in his sickle into the earth, and gathered the vine of the earth, and cast it into the great winepress of the wrath of God."

God is resolute about destroying the works of those who persist in rebellion against His laws and refuse to leave their sinful paths, despite His repeated calls and warnings of impending judgment for both the living and the dead.

The unsaved dead will be resurrected to face judgment by Jesus Christ, the very Word of God they refused to believe and obey. Yet, there is still time to embrace the gospel of salvation. Today, anyone can turn to God and allow the blood of Jesus Christ to cleanse them from the stains of sin. Now is the time to approach Jesus just as you are, for no other moment is guaranteed.

A great multitude already feels God's call, urging them out of a life ensnared by sin and Satan's influence. This moment is the only guaranteed opportunity for anyone to invite Jesus Christ into their lives, transforming them fundamentally from the inside out. God will not abandon anyone who comes to Him broken and repentant, seeking forgiveness for a life lived in defiance of their Creator.

The Bible declares that Satan's purpose is to kill, steal, and destroy (John 10:10). He exploits the sinful nature of humanity to fulfill this agenda. As a relentless adversary, he devises plans to keep mankind in perpetual rebellion against God, destined for destruction. Yet, those living in accordance with God's Word pose a threat to Satan's kingdom. Individuals purified by the blood of Jesus, whose sins have been washed away, remain under His protective covering. These true believers relish the presence of God and are not easily deceived by Satan's machinations.

Brothers and sisters, we must flee even the appearance of evil (1 Thessalonians 5:22). It is crucial for Christians to recognize what evil looks like and not engage in futile attempts to outsmart the devil. We are no match for his cunning and power. Satan, with thousands of years of experience, has honed his skills in deception, destroying many lives through his lies.

Satan requires God's permission to afflict His children, whether in flesh or possessions. To shield ourselves, we must immerse in God's Word, allowing our faith to flourish and protect us from the enemy's fiery darts (Ephesians 6). Without the full armor of God, we are vulnerable and exposed to Satan's potent temptations, which could lead us into sin and estrangement from God. The weapons of our spiritual warfare are mighty through God for the demolition of strongholds (2 Corinthians 10:4).

Every Christian should be familiar with the Word of God to discern Satan's lies and his counterfeit gospel. God expects us to be proactive in our spiritual journey—He will not coddle those who, despite having access to His unadulterated Word, neglect their divine responsibilities. Those unprepared for Jesus's return are setting themselves up for failure, risking eternal separation from God.

We must remember that Satan often masquerades as an angel of light (2 Corinthians 11:14), a "messenger" bearing falsehoods. Since the Garden of Eden, he has been actively promoting his deceptive doctrines, leading astray those who hesitate to fully embrace the true gospel of Jesus Christ. His cunning messages, mingled with elements of truth, ensnare those unfamiliar with God's Word. Tragically, these individuals fall prey to his lies, ultimately finding their names omitted from the Lamb's Book of Life.

Many will remain entrenched in spiritual Babylon, tied to the world's systems. God will abandon them to a reprobate mind because they have stifled the Holy Spirit's work in their lives. These individuals, the unsaved of the world, will accept the deceptive gospel of Satan and his minions—the fallen angels. If you have not yet become a new creation in Christ Jesus, urgently seek God now, so you are not found wanting and clothed in unrighteousness when Jesus returns to take His faithful home to heaven.

Time is short as the world nears its end. The signs, as outlined in Matthew 24 and related scriptures, are becoming evident, pointing to the imminent return of Christ for His elect, His Bride, the true church. By that time, everyone's eternal destiny will have been decided. As stated earlier, all deeds will be tested by fire (1 Corinthians 3:13-15). God's servants are marked by Him (Revelation 7), while those who remain unsaved will bear the mark of the beast (Revelation 13 and 22), making salvation impossible—a stark contrast to some teachings that wrongly suggest a second chance post-Christ's return.

Friend, come to Jesus now. Emulate the five wise virgins who took extra oil for their lamps, remaining vigilant and prepared for their Redeemer's arrival (Matthew 25:1-13). They were filled with the Holy Spirit, ready to meet Jesus. In contrast, the five foolish virgins, lacking sufficient oil, were unprepared. Assuming they had more time, they were caught unready at His return. This illustrates the peril of lacking the Holy Spirit's indwelling—the true light in this dark world.

In these last days, Satan's deceptions will intensify, threatening even the faithful. Yet, God remains the only steadfast anchor, protector, and foundation for His children. Dedicate time to reading, studying, and meditating on God's Word, and maintain a constant prayer life. Satan and his agents are ever observant, seeking to exploit our spiritual strengths and weaknesses to lead us into depravity.

Walking in the Spirit ensures we do not fulfill the desires of the flesh, which are at odds with the Spirit (Galatians 5). These opposing forces prevent us from doing the godly things we wish to do. However, those led by the Spirit will naturally follow God's ways, and the law will no longer bind them—it governs only the lawless and disobedient.

Yielding to temptation grants Satan authority over our lives, manifesting in acts of the flesh such as adultery, fornication, uncleanness, idolatry, hatred, witchcraft, wrath, strife, seditions, heresies, murders, and drunkenness. Conversely, walking with God in the Spirit produces the fruits of righteousness. As children of God in Christ, we are called to crucify our carnal nature through self-denial, embodying the transformative power of the Holy Spirit.

We must remember that if we live by the Spirit, we should also walk by the Spirit, as stated in Galatians 5. The name of the Lord is a strong tower where the righteous find safety (Proverbs 18:10). God will protect His followers, who cling to the Lamb wherever He goes and who uphold the testimony of Jesus, from Satan's deceptions during the imminent great tribulation, foretold by prophecies like those in Matthew 24.

Many Christians today succumb to the devil's torment because they lack the full armor of God and neglect daily communion with the Father.

The distractions of this world often eclipse their spiritual focus, shifting it from heavenly pursuits to earthly ones. Satan needs only a slight opening to wreak havoc in our lives. Therefore, we must live according to the Word and put its teachings into practice.

Jesus exemplified a life of constant prayer and communion with God. As His followers, we must emulate His practices, especially in these perilous times. The urgency for God's people to remain sober, vigilant, and watchful cannot be overstated.

A cosmic battle between good and evil, initiated by Lucifer's rebellion in heaven, continues to rage. Satan's ambition was not just to remain in heaven, but to usurp God's sovereign throne. Michael and his angels clashed with the dragon and his followers in a celestial battle as described in Revelation 12:7. This war over the souls of humanity and the dominion of the universe is driven by Satan's covetous desire for what God created for His own pleasure. Using unorthodox warfare tactics, Satan targets God's obedient children for destruction.

Spiritual lethargy within the church is alarming. Many who profess faith are not actively engaging in the spiritual battle against sin and temptation. They prioritize worldly affairs over the Kingdom's work, allowing the cares and riches of this world to suffocate the Word in their hearts. They avoid confronting their sins and Satan, fearing the personal cost. Such inaction invites Satan to operate unchecked, except when they turn to Scripture and prayer. This passive stance towards spiritual warfare is perilous.

To triumph over sin, we must actively combat Satan's temptations with the Word of God, which should be etched in our hearts. Our spiritual arsenal is formidable, capable of demolishing strongholds and casting down every pretension that sets itself against the knowledge of God (2 Corinthians 10:4-5). Living in faith and victory with Jesus means confronting Satan with the sword of the Spirit, declaring that the Word of God sustains and nourishes us. We are well-prepared and robust in our spiritual health to withstand the devil's schemes.

The ultimate defeat of Satan is already decreed from eternity. As God's children, we must support each other in this spiritual warfare, ensuring that none fall while standing on the frontline against evil.

As we navigate the turbulent times prophesied about, it is crucial to remember that the battle belongs to the Lord, yet the struggle against temptations from the enemy is ours. Satan seeks out the spiritually vulnerable to destroy them. Every true Christian must reach a point in their life where they would rather die a martyr for Christ than succumb to Satan's temptations and sin against God (Mark 8:35). God urges His children to choose life over death (Deuteronomy 30:19).

Our lives must align with the Word of God (Jesus Christ). Every sin is serious in God's eyes, and the penalty for breaking His holy Law is the second death—the eternal destruction of body and soul in the lake of fire. If you are entangled in the sin of adultery or any other transgression, only the blood of Jesus can cleanse you. God invites you to become a new creation, setting you on a path of holy living. Come to Jesus now for a transformative encounter that will change your life forever!

Often, it seems as if Satan has free rein in people's lives because they have unknowingly granted him access. Stubbornness and ego can lead individuals to believe they can resist Satan on their own, yet they find themselves overwhelmed by chaos. This turmoil might indicate unresolved sin giving Satan the leverage to wreak havoc. It's essential to heed God's prompting to confess and repent; otherwise, we remain trapped in confusion and chaos, never experiencing the true freedom Christ offers. For those living in sin, Satan exercises control, robbing them of God's peace.

Satan mimics Christ's actions to deceive God's children with his lies. We are warned that Satan can transform himself into an angel of light, and his ministers into ministers of righteousness (2 Corinthians 11:14-15). Though he may appear as a messenger of God, he is, in truth, a deceitful wolf in sheep's clothing.

Children of God must scrutinize every gospel messenger. Without a deep understanding of the Word, how can we recognize Satan's deceptions? We must study the Scriptures to discern truth from falsehood. According to Isaiah 8:20, if their words do not align with the Word of God, they hold no truth. Thus, each of us must intimately know the Word through the Holy Spirit and live it out.

In the last days, demonic spirits will perform signs and wonders to deceive, as foretold in Matthew 24:24 and Revelation 16:14. They are spirits from the dragon, the beast, and the false prophet, gathering the world for the final battle. Despite his attempts to emulate the divine, Satan's power is limited. He can never attain the authority of God; his true nature remains that of the dragon, the beast, and the false prophet, all manifestations of his deceitful character.

God has endowed us with faith, a gift from Himself through His Word, enabling us to trust in Him—the only true and wise God. The Bible assures us that it is impossible for the elect to be deceived by Satan, his false ministers, or his false prophets during the great tribulation. The elect are sealed with the righteousness of Christ in their foreheads, embodying the character of God. They are purified through the blood of Jesus, upholding the commandments of God and bearing the testimony of Jesus Christ (Matthew 24:24, Revelation 7:3, Revelation 14:12).

An important clarification is necessary concerning a prevalent misunderstanding among some Christians. It has become fashionable in certain circles to emphasize "the blood of Christ" more than Christ Himself, from whom the blood derives its sanctifying power. The blood of Christ is indeed powerful because it comes from Him—holy and righteous. However, Christ's death, His blood, and His resurrection are equally vital to the redemption of the world. We cannot dissect His sacrifice into components, elevating one above the others as more effective. The Bible does not support such division; teachings that suggest otherwise are misleading. Satan, ever the deceiver, uses such distortions to confuse and lead astray those called to be God's chosen.

Satan's influence is potent. He wields his power over those who serve him, yet his machinations are futile against the true children of God. We must remain vigilant, examining the fruits of those who claim divine authority, using the Word of God not to judge, but to discern the truth of their claims.

Leadership, whether in homes, churches, or governmental positions, carries significant responsibility. The Bible illustrates this through figures such as Adam, King Saul, and Moses, each held accountable by God for their leadership. The history of Israel, as chronicled in the books of Kings and Chronicles, shows many kings who led in defiance of God, engaging in idolatrous worship and demonic rituals, bringing great tribulation upon the nation through their apostate leadership.

As followers of Christ, we are called to emulate His example of true leadership. Whether leading a family, a congregation, or a community, we must adopt the servant-hearted attitude demonstrated by Christ during His earthly ministry. Being mission-minded for the cause of God is essential for every Christian. Proverbs 14:34 reminds us, "Righteousness exalteth a nation, but sin is a reproach to any people." God does not call the equipped; He equips those He calls, preparing and empowering us to fulfill our divine mandate.

CHAPTER 12

GOD IS TO BE WORSHIPED

Philippians 3:3 encapsulates a profound spiritual transformation: "For we are the circumcision, which worship God in the spirit, rejoice in Christ Jesus, and have no confidence in the flesh." This metaphorical circumcision of the heart represents God removing the stony unbelief and rebellion that prevent sinners from truly knowing Him.

Through this divine intervention, individuals are reborn with a new spirit inclined solely towards serving God. This transformative process is what it means to be born again.

The power to accept the gospel of Jesus Christ is a gift from God, who also reveals to us that we have been buried with Christ through baptism and raised with Him through the power of the Father (Romans 1:16, Ephesians 2, Colossians 2). Consequently, true worship emanates from this new spirit within every believer, aligning with Jesus' teaching that "God is a Spirit, and those who worship Him must worship in spirit and truth" (John 4:24).

Contrastingly, the carnal nature of mankind, or the flesh, is inclined towards sin and does not seek to worship God. Fleshly worship is driven by emotions and feelings, which are inherently unstable. This vulnerability is why Satan targets our fleshly weaknesses, knowing well that victory is assured for him in these battles.

A spiritually dead person, disconnected from any relationship with God, cannot truly know or worship Him, as they are devoid of life and understanding (Ecclesiastes 9:5).

Isaiah 29:13 warns of worship that is merely lip service, devoid of heartfelt devotion: "The Lord said, 'These people come near to me with their mouth and honor me with their lips, but their hearts are far from me. Their worship of me is based on merely human rules they have been taught.'" This sentiment is echoed in Matthew 15:8-9, where Jesus emphasizes that true worship cannot be divorced from the heart's true condition. He knows when worship is genuine and when it is performed as a mere formality.

True worship involves more than just words; it requires a life that continually glorifies God regardless of circumstances. James 1:26-27 calls for worship that is reflective of a godly lifestyle, not one focused on self or empty rituals. Worship must be an active, consistent practice that glorifies God in all aspects of life, proving that Christ is Lord of all, both in trials and triumphs.

The Psalmist David models this in Psalm 34:1-2, declaring, "I will bless the Lord at all times; His praise will always be on my lips. My soul will boast in the Lord; let the humble hear and rejoice." Here, David shows that true praise springs from the soul, transcending all life's challenges. This ordered way of living leaves no room for spiritual idleness or for Satan to influence our thoughts with his deceptions.

True worship involves total submission to God's ways, relinquishing every aspect of our lives to His will. We cannot expect to experience the fullness of God's promises while living in rebellion or as covenant breakers. Have you ever pondered why certain areas of your life are fraught with difficulties? It's often because we haven't fully trusted God to strengthen our weaknesses, allowing us to be liberated from them. Although we acknowledge God's ability to sustain us, letting go completely can be challenging. Total surrender on the altar of sacrifice, however, invites a life free from worry—though not from challenges—in Christ Jesus. God's grace, manifested in our weakness, becomes our strength and sufficiency through life's trials.

Worshiping God means to love Him with all our heart, soul, strength, and mind (Deuteronomy 6:5 and Matthew 22:37). Love, in its true form, is patient, kind, enduring, and hopeful (1 Corinthians 13). It requires that we relinquish control, aligning our life's blueprint with God's Word, and acting on His infinite wisdom without doubt. Obedience to God's commands invariably leads to success in all life's aspects.

God embodies love—He is its very definition. Love is an action, exemplified when God gave His only Son for us, reflecting the greatest gift of all—Himself (John 3:16). God's love is unconditional, free from any strings (1 John 4:8). Jesus' words in John 14:15, "If you love me, keep my commandments," underscore that genuine love for God is demonstrated through obedience.

Understanding and keeping God's commandments involves diligent engagement with Scripture. We must explore the Bible to discern both the dos and don'ts as outlined by God, letting His Spirit guide our understanding and actions. Regular scriptural study fortifies us, enabling a lifestyle that honors God, no matter the circumstances. Challenges may arise as divine tools, sculpting our faith and dependence on God, ensuring we credit Him for our victories.

Like a cedar planted by God, our roots must grow deep so that when life's storms rage, we remain steadfast—not uprooted or shattered. The tempests of life, while they may strip away some leaves, serve to shake off detrimental habits and cleanse us of redundancies. God uses these trials to break our willful spirits, leading to humility and renewal. When the storm passes, and we've been realigned by God's hands, all glory and praise rightfully return to Him.

As we emerge cleansed and renewed, our worship becomes pure, proclaiming Christ as the sole object of our devotion. Let us resist the seeds of discouragement and doubt that threaten our worship. We deepen our connection with God through consistent and diligent study of the Bible. Living rightly before God ensures that our prayers, aligned with His will, are answered.

The intensity of Satan's attacks often signals proximity to spiritual breakthroughs. Jesus Himself endured severe trials as He approached the culmination of His redemptive mission, yet His unwavering connection with the Father sustained Him.

Just as Jesus relied on the Father during His earthly ministry, particularly in facing Satan's relentless attacks, we too must depend on God for sustenance. Christ's example teaches us never to waver from the path God has set before us. Even in the depths of trial, God's presence remains steadfast; though we may stray, He never abandons us. This enduring promise underscores that the race for righteousness is not won by the swift or the strong but by those who persevere through every challenge until Christ's return. The victory is already ours in Christ, although Satan fails to grasp this truth. Do not succumb to despair, for your destiny is secure in Christ, authored by God Himself through His sacrificial love.

Romans 8:28 assures us that all things work together for good for those who love God and are called according to His purpose. This divine orchestration is not subject to human or demonic wills but solely to God's sovereign plan. Our trials serve to reshape us into His image, for we were created to reflect His likeness. Initially marred by sin, our journey becomes a transformative process under God's masterful hands, molding us through the discomfort of change into refined children of God, as Ephesians 2:10 affirms: "For we are his workmanship, created in Christ Jesus for good works, which God prepared beforehand, that we should walk in them."

In John 15, Jesus describes Himself as the true vine, with God the Father as the vinedresser who prunes us to bear more fruit. This analogy clarifies that spiritual growth involves divine pruning, which is neither arbitrary nor influenced by the enemy. It is a deliberate process to remove the toxins of sin and enhance our fruitfulness. As branches, we do not control the pruning process; it is the Father who determines the necessary cuts for growth. Abiding in Christ ensures that our lives are fruitful, and His words in us empower us to fulfill His will effectively.

If you find yourself in seemingly catastrophic difficulties, feeling alone and overwhelmed, remember that God cares deeply. Jesus Christ stands ready to assist you, offering immediate help in times of need. No situation is too dire for His intervention. He has been with you through every stage of your life, orchestrating events to draw you closer to Him. Now, as you face this tumultuous period, God invites you to recognize His guiding hand.

In moments of despair, when life seems out of control and directionless, God remains your steadfast helper. His attributes—faithfulness, mercy, compassion, and patience—ensure that He will not let you be overwhelmed by the enemy's schemes. This realization should bring comfort and encourage reliance on God, for a life led without His guidance is bound to falter. Let God lead, and you will find your way out of chaos into peace and purpose.

Your status or condition in this life does not define how God sees you, for He is capable of mending every broken aspect of your existence. What truly matters to God is that you worship Him wholly, in every facet of your life, without reservation. True worshipers who engage with God in spirit and in truth receive His blessings abundantly—so much so that they overflow and must be shared with others.

Worship involves not just our words and songs, but also our time, talents, and treasures. God calls us to honor Him with everything He has entrusted to us, from our financial resources to our abilities and possessions. The magnitude of our net worth is irrelevant to God; what counts is our recognition that everything we possess comes from Him.

Moreover, God desires our complete devotion, affirming His preeminence in our lives. We are to demonstrate that nothing is held back from Him, as He declares Himself a jealous God (Exodus 20:5). This act of worship extends beyond our personal lives into our finances, careers, marriages, and families. True worship means entering the holy of holies beyond the veil of separation, singing hymns and songs of praise and deliverance, and expressing heartfelt gratitude for God's perpetual goodness and mercy amidst our challenges.

Many face acute trials—loss of loved ones, employment, homes, or health crises. These moments may seem insurmountable in the natural realm, but rest assured, God shelters you under His wings. Like Christ, who trusted the Father through the excruciating pain of the cross, we must look beyond our current sufferings. Christ, "for the joy set before him endured the cross, scorning its shame, and sat down at the right hand of the throne of God" (Hebrews 12:2).

You may not understand the reasons behind the overwhelming challenges you face, nor why God permits them. Yet, it is crucial to maintain faith and trust in Him throughout these refining processes. Resist any inclination to doubt or surrender, regardless of the pain involved in transformation. God meticulously controls every aspect of the trials you endure, knowing precisely what you can handle and equipping you for the battle of faith.

Do not allow Satan to distract you from focusing on God, the ultimate healer and resolver of all life's difficulties. Christ understands your struggles more profoundly than anyone else could, having ordained these moments before the world was formed. Though your faith and trust may be tested, God has already prepared a pathway to victory. He initiated this storm in your life, knowing that with His strength, you can endure and emerge with a fortified faith capable of extinguishing the enemy's fiercest attacks.

Always trust in God—He navigates you through every tempest, ensuring that each trial enhances your faith and prepares you for greater spiritual victories.

CHAPTER 13

PRAYER

Prayer is an integral part of worship, a sacred encounter where we meet and communicate with God face-to-face. It's in prayer that we recognize God as the central figure in our lives. This divine communication should be a vital practice for every believer, not only to present our troubles but to express gratitude for both victories and disappointments because of God's involvement in our lives.

Prayer transcends mere petitions for our desires or an attempt to persuade God to remedy every issue on demand. True prayer is not about making demands on God as if He were a genie granting wishes. Instead, it's a sincere, heartfelt dialogue that honors God for His presence and providence, acknowledging that without Him, we would be lost amid our chaos.

Our prayers should focus on spiritual growth and extend to intercedory petitions on behalf of others, including those in our nation without a relationship with God. We should seek divine wisdom to navigate all situations wisely. Prayer is not a tool for avoiding the consequences of deliberate wrongdoings; God, in His infinite mercy, is gracious but He is not to be manipulated or deceived.

For those unfamiliar with Jesus as Savior and Lord, enduring the consequences of sin, there is hope. God offers cleansing and deliverance through sincere confession and repentance. He desires to be our closest ally, respected and honored in our relationship with Him because of His absolute holiness.

Prayer should be a time of intimate and sacred communion with God, where every believer's plea should echo the psalmist's request: "Search me, O God, and know my heart; test me and know my anxious thoughts. See if there is any offensive way in me, and lead me in the way everlasting"

(Psalm 139:23-24). We should consistently seek to align our desires with God's will and request the fortitude to obey His commandments.

In our prayers, we should aspire to reflect Christ's mind and character, becoming beacons of His light to our neighbors. Faith-driven prayer acts as the essence of true worship, maintaining our spiritual connection with God. As Luke 18:1 advises, we should always pray and not give up, ensuring that we remain steadfast and unafraid of worldly distresses. This continuous communion with God shields us from the overwhelming worries that plague the world and the misguided paths nations often take.

While disobedience may lead to afflictions and the natural consequences of sin, God remains ever ready to extend forgiveness and mercy to those who earnestly seek Him. Prayer keeps us tethered to God's protective grace, ensuring that even when we face life's storms, we are never beyond the reach of His redeeming love.

God is acutely aware of every scheme devised by the forces of darkness against His people. He hears the prayers of the righteous seeking deliverance from the clutches of Satan's armies. Sometimes, it might feel as though God is distant during our trials, but by maintaining our faith amidst chaos, we experience His salvation as a timely aid in our distress. Even if we do not visibly see divine forces encircling our adversaries, we must trust by faith that the Lord will deliver us unscathed from the snares of the evil one.

As Jesus approached the hour of His greatest suffering, He remained in constant communion with the Father. Facing the daunting prospect of bearing the world's sins, Christ prayed fervently, desiring another way yet submitting to God's will above His own (Matthew 26:39). His ultimate act of obedience—commendation of His spirit into the Father's hands at the cross (Luke 23:46)—exemplifies perfect submission to God's divine plan.

God honors such obedience, urging us to surrender every aspect of our lives—both joys and trials—to His sovereign care. It was God's purpose, not Satan's, that Christ should sacrifice His life to redeem humanity. Despite Satan's attempts to thwart the crucifixion, God's plans prevailed, illustrating that no adversarial design can withstand His power.

As God's children, we should not be preoccupied with the dire forecasts for our world or societal decay. Our primary concern should be proclaiming the Gospel of Jesus Christ to the unsaved. We are called to be fervent intercessors, praying that God's Word reaches every corner of the globe and touches the hearts of those yet to embrace Christ as Savior.

The church must persist in prayer for those still enslaved by darkness, that they may choose life in Christ.

God's people are not meant to live in isolation, shielded from the world's troubles. We are called to active service, helping others discover the transformative love of God that rescued us from sin. Each believer is to be an aroma of Christ, a sweet fragrance of His love to the world. This cannot be achieved from afar; we must engage directly with the world God redeemed us from.

True Christian living is not a passive observance but a call to action. Every believer is tasked with the Great Commission, to be laborers in God's kingdom. We cannot consider the spread of the Gospel as the responsibility of only a select few; it is a mandate for all. Once we were distant from God, lost in our transgressions, until we received the life-altering message of Christ's salvation.

Now, empowered by that same transformative Gospel, we are commissioned to extend this message of hope to a world desperate for redemption. As representatives of Christ, we have no other hands, feet, and voices but our own to carry this eternal message across the globe. This mission is not optional—it is the essence of our calling as followers of Christ, saved to serve in His kingdom.

God is fully aware of every scheme devised against His people by agents of darkness, and He hears the righteous cry out for deliverance. While it may sometimes feel as though God is distant during our tribulations, maintaining faith amid chaos assures us of His saving presence when we need it most. Even if divine forces aren't visibly surrounding our adversaries, we must trust by faith that the Lord will deliver us from evil unscathed.

God witnessed the agony of Christ as He prepared to lay down His life, offering the perfect atonement for the sins of humanity. In His profound distress, Christ earnestly prayed for another way, yet submitted to the Father's will, ensuring the completion of the divine plan of reconciliation (Matthew 26:39). Through His unwavering obedience and ultimate sacrifice, Christ demonstrated the depth of divine love and commitment to God's will.

As followers of Jesus, we are called to a similar path of obedience and sacrifice. We are to surrender every aspect of our lives to God, trusting Him with both our joys and our struggles. Christ's journey from darkness to light was not orchestrated by Satan but was a divine design by God the Father, to redeem His lost sheep and cleanse us from sin through Christ's sacrifice.

As the disciples were instructed to leave their nets and follow Jesus to become fishers of men, so too are all Christians commanded to actively spread the Gospel (Matthew 4:19). The Church is appointed as the watchman, tasked with announcing the imminent return of Christ and the urgent need for reconciliation with God. This mission involves stepping into environments that may not always be welcoming or safe because, by nature, humanity is resistant to the message of salvation.

Christ's directive to be as lambs among wolves underscores the risks involved in evangelism (Luke 10:1-12). Yet, He assures us of divine protection and empowerment to overcome all adversities, promising that nothing shall harm us as we carry out our mission. The fields are ripe for harvest, but the laborers are few; therefore, we must pray earnestly for more workers to join this crucial effort.

We cannot afford to be passive or selective in whom we witness to; our calling is to go wherever there are souls in need of the Gospel. This work transcends personal safety and comfort, demanding a commitment to serve wherever God calls us. As ambassadors for Christ, we are entrusted with a message that has the power to transform lives and prepare people for the Second Coming of Jesus.

In these critical times, every Christian is called to be an active participant in the Great Commission, spreading the Gospel not just locally but globally. We must be vigilant, prayerful, and dedicated to this cause, knowing that time is short and the return of Christ is near.

As we continue to navigate the complexities of the world and face the challenges that lie ahead, let us remain steadfast in our faith and diligent in our service, empowered by the knowledge that God is with us, guiding and protecting us as we work to expand His kingdom.

Prayer is essential in worship, providing a sacred space where we commune face-to-face with God. It's an opportunity to affirm His central role in our lives. While some Christians might pray for the avoidance of life's challenges, it is more spiritually fruitful to seek strength to endure them. True faith grows in the crucible of adversity, and because we are in Christ and His Spirit resides within us, we possess God's power to serve others fearlessly, knowing that Satan is a defeated foe.

At times, we may not know precisely what to pray for, but the Holy Spirit aids us by interceding with unspeakable groanings, aligning our desires with God's will (Romans 8:26-27). Prayer, guided by the Holy

Spirit, transcends mere articulation of needs—it involves a heart-to-heart communion with God, discussing what He has inspired within us.

True prayer focuses not only on our needs but extends to the needs of others, embracing the challenges they face. It is about seeking closeness to God and interceding for the global community of believers as instructed in Ephesians 6:18. God, in His generosity, withholds no good thing from us, inviting us to approach Him with a spirit-led heart rather than fleshly desires.

Meaningful prayer also involves seeking purification from sin, aspiring to become more Christ-like. Sometimes, this means praying for others, even those who oppose us, reflecting Christ's command to love our enemies. God's responses to our prayers may vary—He knows best what we need and provides accordingly, though not always in the ways we expect. This misalignment can lead to doubts or frustrations when His answers do not match our desires.

It's crucial to recognize that God cannot be manipulated by selfish or insincere prayers. He does not entertain prayers stemming from a manipulative spirit. Such prayers are contrary to His nature, as He is holy and righteous. Those who engage in manipulative prayers must repent before it's too late, as harboring sin can obstruct our spiritual communication with God. Psalm 66:18 warns, "If I regard iniquity in my heart, the Lord will not hear me."

God desires heartfelt communication from His children. He delights in our thanksgiving and praises, finding joy when we approach Him with genuine intent. The prayers of the righteous are indeed a sweet aroma to God, pleasing and acceptable in His sight.

God's responses to our prayers are always aligned with His divine will and timing, not our immediate desires or schedules. He encourages us to pray for our needs and the needs of others, urging us to become vessels of His goodness and mercy. When our prayers align with God's will, they become powerful instruments of change, not just in our lives but in the lives of those around us.

Our sincere prayers are shielded from the understanding of Satan. They are communicated in a spiritual language that only God can comprehend, protected by the Holy Spirit. This ensures that our deepest, purest petitions are known only to God. Vain repetitions and theatrical prayers are of no value; God is moved only by the sincerity of our hearts and the honesty of our words.

Many believers have testified to God's faithfulness, having experienced deliverance through heartfelt prayer. As stated in Psalm 22:4-5, those who cry out to God in trust will not be forsaken. Similarly, Matthew 6:31-32 reminds us not to worry about our basic needs like food and clothing because God knows and provides for our necessities. Worrying about these things often reflects a lack of trust in God's provision.

Philippians 4:6-7 teaches us to approach God with everything by prayer and supplication with thanksgiving, ensuring peace that surpasses all understanding guards our hearts and minds in Christ Jesus. This divine peace is a gift that helps us remain calm and confident, irrespective of external circumstances.

Yet, the modern desire for instant gratification can sometimes hinder our spiritual patience and trust in God. We live in an age of immediate results, from fast food to instant messaging, which can skew our expectations when it comes to prayer. We must remember that divine timing is perfect and rarely conforms to our personal deadlines. Rushing God or becoming disillusioned when answers don't arrive on our timetable only leads to frustration and increased anxiety.

When we try to solve problems on our own without waiting for God's guidance, we often complicate matters further. This impatience can disrupt the beautiful plans God has for us, plans that unfold not within our hurried timelines but at a divine pace meant to bring about the best outcomes for our growth and His glory.

Therefore, instead of succumbing to the pressures of an on-demand culture, let us cultivate patience and steadfast faith. Let us trust that God hears every prayer and that His timing in answering those prayers is always meant to bring about greater good than we could imagine. Remember, God is not bound by our schedules; He transcends time and sees the end from the beginning.

In your prayers, continue to seek God's presence with a spirit of gratitude for what He has already accomplished in your life. Embrace the waiting period as a time for growth and deepening trust. God is always at work, even when we do not perceive it, weaving our stories into His grand tapestry of grace and redemption.

Living in a fast-paced, instant gratification society often influences our expectations of divine response. We may approach God with urgency and impatience, expecting swift solutions to our prayers, yet forgetting that God operates outside the constraints of human time and disorder.

Our chaotic lifestyles and last-minute pleas do not dictate His actions; rather, God responds in His perfect timing, always aligning His answers with His will and our ultimate good.

God calls us to prioritize Him in all aspects of life, not to turn to Him only as a last resort. By starting each day in His presence and committing our plans to Him, we can mitigate the chaos and cultivate a life of deeper peace and fulfillment. It is essential to resist the distractions and discouragements that Satan may place in our path, using the truth of God's Word to fortify our minds and hearts against doubt and fear.

When we pray, we must do so with a spirit of thanksgiving, praising God even before we see the manifestation of His answers. This attitude of gratitude aligns our spirit with God's nature and opens the door for His blessings to flow more abundantly into our lives. True prayer involves not only asking for our needs but also celebrating what God has already done and will continue to do. We must trust that God has heard us and that He will fulfill His promises in His own perfect timing.

Moreover, the privilege of prayer is not limited by location or circumstance. Through Christ's sacrifice, we have direct access to God, allowing us to communicate with Him anytime and anywhere. This constant availability invites us to engage in continuous dialogue with our Heavenly Father, bringing our praises, our worries, and our desires directly to His throne.

We are called to be vigilant in prayer, not just for personal needs but also for our families, communities, and the world. Our intercessory prayers are a powerful tool for change, both in the lives of others and in societal structures. Instead of criticizing or condemning, we should use our access to God to seek His intervention and grace for those around us and for those in leadership, regardless of their faults.

In essence, prayer is a profound communion with God that empowers us, transforms us, and uplifts those around us. It is through prayer that we tap into the boundless resources of heaven, allowing God's power to manifest in our lives for His glory. Let us then approach God with open hearts and hands lifted in holiness, free from wrath and doubt, fully assured that our prayers are heard and answered by our faithful Father.

As followers of Jesus, we are called not just to receive His grace but to actively extend it to others, embodying His love and compassion in a world rife with judgment and rejection. We must remember that once, we too were distant from God, entrenched in sin and rebellion. It was the prayers and the grace of God, channeled through others' faithfulness, that drew us out of darkness. Therefore, we have no grounds to deem anyone beyond redemption or to exhibit impatience and disdain towards those struggling in sin.

Christians are to be ambassadors of Christ's unconditional love and forgiveness, demonstrating humility and patience in our interactions. We are not judges but witnesses of the life-changing power of the gospel. Our lives should be open books, illustrating the transformative work of God's grace and the true essence of being born again.

The Gospel compels us to be lights in the darkness, to be the salt that preserves and enhances. We must live out the teachings of Jesus, not only in our private lives but publicly, serving as living testimonies to His mercy and power. As Daniel 12:3 inspires, those who lead many to righteousness shine like the stars forever.

Therefore, let us not shy away from praying anywhere—at home, in public spaces, or in our workplaces. Our prayer should not be hidden but should reflect our confidence in God's provision and protection. This visible faith can be a beacon to others, drawing them towards a relationship with God.

Moreover, it is essential to maintain a posture of prayer that is inclusive and intercessory. We are called to pray for everyone—those on Wall Street and those on Main Street—reflecting God's impartiality and His desire that all should come to repentance. Our prayers can bridge gaps and break down barriers, serving as a conduit for God's grace to flow into the lives of others.

In every moment and with every breath, let us be relentless in our commitment to prayer, fearless in our faith, and unashamed in our devotion. Let the fragrance of our praise permeate our surroundings, drawing others to recognize the beauty of a life committed to serving God. Let us remember that every life is precious in His eyes, worth every effort to save. This is the essence of our calling as God's children—to pray without ceasing, to live out the gospel in word and deed, and to ensure that our lives reflect the grace and truth of Jesus Christ.

By living and praying in this manner, we not only fulfill our divine mandate but also contribute to a legacy of faith that transcends generations, impacting lives for eternity. Let us seize every opportunity to demonstrate God's love, ensuring that no one we encounter ever doubts the extent of His reach or the depth of His compassion.

In conclusion, our walk with God and our life of prayer are central to living out the Gospel authentically. As disciples of Christ, we must exhibit a life that harmoniously aligns with God's Word, serving as living testimonies to His power and grace. This requires humility, diligence, and a constant connection to God through prayer, ensuring that our actions and lifestyle genuinely reflect His love and teachings.

Being bold in faith means displaying confidence in God's promises and providence, not through arrogance or self-righteous displays, but through a spirit of meekness and piety that draws others to Christ. Our lives should encourage others to explore and eventually embrace the transformative journey of faith. This does not mean imposing our beliefs but living in such a way that our faith naturally invites curiosity and respect.

Furthermore, as we navigate through life's challenges, it is crucial to prioritize our relationship with God. Let us not allow the busyness of life or the pursuit of worldly things to distract us from our spiritual duties. Regular, heartfelt communion with God is essential, not just in times of need but as a continual practice. This connection is our lifeline, sustaining us through trials and guiding us in truth.

When we find ourselves straying from this path, it is vital to seek God's help to realign our priorities. He is always ready to draw us back and deepen our commitment to Him. Remember, God does not just listen to our prayers; He looks at the heart behind them. Prayers driven by selfish motives or material envy will not bear the fruit we hope for. Instead, we must approach God with pure intentions, seeking not only His blessings but also His guidance and correction.

Every unanswered prayer or delay is an opportunity to reflect on our motives and desires, allowing God to mold our character and desires to better suit His will. These moments teach us to rely on God more fully, recognizing that our true fulfillment and peace come from His presence, not from the transient things of this world.

As we continue our journey as Christians, let us remember to live out the truth of the Gospel with integrity and love. Let us be diligent in prayer, generous in love, and steadfast in faith. By doing so, we not only enrich our own lives but also shine as beacons of hope and sources of inspiration for others to find their way to God.

Through such a life, we fulfill the great commission to spread the Gospel, demonstrating through our example that every life is indeed precious to God, worthy of His love, and capable of experiencing His transformative grace.

Wait on God When You Pray

Some professed Christians claim we are blessed by God, even when the gains are clearly obtained through ungodly means. This behavior often stems from impatience and a lack of faith in God's timing and answers to our prayers. Eager to impress, many fall into deep debt and trouble, simply to keep up with the Joneses.

There are those among us who form unwise alliances with ungodly individuals, only to find themselves entangled with serpents and scorpions—metaphors for harmful consequences that could have been fatal. Hastily pursued desires leave some scarred and burned because they did not wait for God's provision. Additionally, some acquire things God does not intend for us, knowing these could lead us to idolatry. Our Heavenly Father loves us too deeply to watch us self-destruct with distractions that could sever our connection with Him. He desires us to consult Him before pursuing things that could lead us astray, always wanting what's best for us—treasures of heaven.

Some self-identified Christians boldly challenge God's justice by indulging in sinful acts, curious if they will face immediate consequences. When punishment does not come swiftly, they plunge deeper into sin. Yet, scripture teaches that God is slow to anger, full of long-suffering and compassion, giving us opportunities to repent. His mercy often spares the guilty from immediate wrath.

Listening to Satan, many are drawn away from God by their own desires and greed. These individuals prioritize their fleshly urges over spiritual guidance, losing focus on the divine influence that teaches them to recognize and flee from evil. They are unwilling to endure even short-term afflictions, believing the pain too great to bear. However, we cannot fulfill fleshly desires and hold onto Jesus simultaneously; one must yield. Demonic strongholds remain unbroken while sin is clutched tightly. Only through Jesus Christ can we be truly freed from sin's grasp.

Rebuking Satan is futile if one maintains alliances with the enemy. The power to effectively rebuke comes from being immersed in the Word of God, earnest prayer, and genuine worship. Divine strength manifests when we confess and repent our sins to God and are baptized into Jesus Christ by the power of the Holy Spirit—not into a specific church or denomination. Christ leads us to the right congregation, where God's Word is preached and taught purely and without alteration. No church or denomination holds the exclusive authority to baptize into their own doctrines; God, through

Christ, owns the true church—His children, over whom He presides as the ultimate authority. The church's mandate from God is clear: to proclaim the gospel of Jesus Christ to the unsaved, baptizing them in the name of the Godhead (Father, Son, and Holy Spirit).

Seeking God's Guidance in Relationships

Many of us claim God has answered our prayers for a spouse, even when we know deep down that our relationships were not divinely inspired but born of lust. When seeking a lifelong partner, it is crucial to pray earnestly for God's direction and to wait patiently for His guidance. Forming relationships lightly can lead to profound emotional distress.

Some women, both young and older—who ought to know better—compromise their values by choosing partners based solely on physical attributes. Such superficial bases for relationships often lead to significant strife, as they mistake outward appearances for genuine love.

Do not let physical desires or shallow thinking override the wisdom and discernment God provides. It is essential to allow God to lead your decisions in choosing a partner. This advice applies equally to young men, many of whom rush into relationships, drawn by physical attraction without discerning the true nature of their feelings. Remember, just because someone catches your eye doesn't mean it's love. Often, we insist on our desires against divine advice, leading to significant errors.

We sometimes decide what we want before consulting God, hoping His will aligns with ours out of impatience and stubbornness. However, God knows best and may block our misguided plans to teach us the importance of His timing. He might allow us to experience certain challenges—not to destroy us but to use them as lessons in wisdom and patience.

God wants more for His children than relationships based merely on physical attraction. Love transcends superficial measurements like 36-24-30. Pray for wisdom and the spirit of discernment. It's a misconception among some single Christian women that God is indifferent to their needs, prompting them to take matters into their own hands. This impatience can lead to spiritual blindness, making it difficult to avoid the snares set by Satan.

From my own experiences, I've learned that hasty decisions often result in emotional scars. But through His Word, God has patiently healed these self-inflicted wounds. I once thought I knew better than God, but I didn't understand life's harsh realities or the cunning of this world as well as I believed. We all need God's counsel and wisdom to navigate life without suffering irreparable damage.

Many seek completeness in a mate when, in truth, completeness should first be found in Christ. Once united with God, all other good things—including the right partner—will follow for those who trust and wait on Him. "Seek first the kingdom of God and His righteousness, and all these things will be added to you." After praying and patiently waiting, your faith will grow, setting a foundation for fulfilling relationships. However, those in haste to experience the joys meant for marriage may end up facing unintended consequences instead of realizing their dreams and hopes.

The Consequences of Impatience and the Power of Divine Timing

Many believers have unfortunately abandoned the divine purposes for which they were created due to impatience and hasty decisions. The dreams they once held dear remain unfulfilled because they did not seek God's guidance or wait for His perfect response.

Remember, brothers and sisters, you are recreated in God's image to reflect His grace to others. As a child of God, you are valued far beyond your physical appearance. God desires to bless you with the best He has to offer. There is no need to compromise your integrity or settle out of desperation as time passes. Elevate your standards to excellence, and God will reward you with His finest.

For my Christian sisters feeling left behind as friends marry: remember, you are like an apple of gold on a platter of silver. God has a perfect timing for revealing the spouse He has chosen for you. Trust in God's timing, and He will bring your "Isaac," the promised husband, into your life.

Prayerfully wait on God, for only He can fulfill all your dreams. Even if you feel that much has been lost, God is ready to enrich you with His grace, mercy, and favor. Remember, God is the potter; we are the clay. Should we mar ourselves with sin, through confession and repentance, Christ is ready to reshape us into new vessels pleasing to Him.

God specializes in mending broken lives. Continue to thank Him after you pray, and patiently await the husband He has uniquely designed for you. This person won't be perfect, but he will be God-fearing and perfectly suited for you. God is your divine matchmaker, and He acts in His own perfect timing.

To our young men and those older who should act with wisdom: avoid violating your own integrity and the innocence of others with pursuits born from lust. Engaging with the metaphorical Delilahs and Jezebels for fleeting pleasure can lead to lifelong pain. Even if the forbidden fruit looks appealing, it is often rotten at its core. When we ignore God's guidance, our impatient actions lead to dire consequences.

Without repentance, God's judgment remains over the guilty. We can achieve so much more with God than we can through sinful desires. Men, do not forsake the dreams and purposes God has placed within you. If you seek a wife, pray and wait patiently. If it aligns with God's will, He will send you your "Rachel" in due time. First, God wants you complete in Him—intimately connected and embodying the character of Jesus Christ—before you seek completeness in a spouse. He prepares you to be a God-fearing husband, just as Christ is to His church.

Among those professing faith in Jesus, some have been entangled in scandals and accusations of sexual misconduct within the church—from pulpit ministers to lay members. Whether they serve on the usher board, in the choir, or in church leadership, it is crucial to understand: God is neither blind nor absent. He is merciful and long-suffering, giving us the chance to turn from our sins.

The Inevitability of Divine Judgment

Many believe that because the consequences of their sins do not manifest immediately, they have evaded punishment for their immoral acts. However, God's judgment persists over the guilty and unrepentant sinners. Such individuals may convince themselves they are exempt from accountability because they handle the sacred Word of God and serve His people—assuming they were genuinely chosen for this holy service. Yet, it is this very Word, sacred and holy, that they read and preach, which will judge them if they do not turn away from their sins.

Recall the sobering episode of Aaron's sons, who offered unauthorized fire before the Lord (Leviticus 10:1–2). Their presumption and disrespect were met with fatal consequences. We must remember, to whom much is given, much is required. Those privileged to serve God's people must never abuse the trust placed in them. Yet, some become spiritually blind, abandoning reason and common sense, foolishly believing they can persist in sin without repercussion. They fail to recognize that they are amassing evidence of their own rebellion against God.

The seeds of evil we sow will inevitably bear fruit unless we repent swiftly. As brothers and sisters in faith, we must continually pray to be kept from temptation and sin, both against God and against others. All sin, without exception, will face severe consequences under God's judgment.

God's Counsel to Husbands

God has given explicit instructions on how husbands should treat their wives, as stated in 1 Peter 3:7: "Likewise, husbands, live with your wives in an understanding way, showing honor to the woman as the weaker vessel, since they are heirs with you of the grace of life, so that your prayers may not be hindered." Have you ever wondered why sometimes your prayers seem unanswered? It could be due to bitterness toward your wife. Christ does not harbor bitterness toward His church; He embodies love and forgiveness, patience and kindness. Even when the church, His bride, sins, God offers mercy and forgiveness upon our confession and repentance.

As husbands, we are called to emulate Christ in all aspects of life. He is our model of true godliness. We must be loving, even when it feels challenging and those around us seem unlovable. Husbands should be the fragrance of Christ within their families, learning to love as God loves. 1 John 4:16 teaches us, "And so we know and rely on the love God has for us. God is love. Whoever lives in love lives in God, and God in them." This requires us to mold our characters after Christ, transformed by the renewal of our minds to exhibit God's good, acceptable, and perfect will.

As Christ loved the church unconditionally—sacrificing His life to redeem her from sin—so should husbands love their wives. Despite our flaws and failings that provoke God's anger, His boundless love restrains Him from immediate judgment. If we profess love for our wives, we must demonstrate it actively. While wives also have responsibilities toward their husbands, as Ephesians 5:22 instructs, "Wives, submit yourselves unto your own husbands, as unto the Lord," this passage serves as a reminder of mutual respect and love required in marriage.

Seeking God in Every Situation

In both our triumphs and our trials, it is crucial to seek God through His Word and prayer for guidance on how to navigate life's challenges. God, who created us, knows us intimately—better than anyone else could. Why wouldn't we want a deep relationship with our Creator, who holds all knowledge about us?

As children of the Most High God, we should avoid dwelling on complaints about life's difficulties. Achieving success is rarely a smooth journey; it often involves overcoming substantial challenges. To succeed, we must be anchored in God's Word, ready to unlearn destructive behaviors and adopt those that bear the fruit of the Spirit. True success comes from being active doers of the Word, not merely listeners.

God uses our trials and disappointments to prepare us for the blessings and favor He plans to pour into our lives. Each challenge is an opportunity for growth and a testament to His providential care.

Enduring Struggles with Divine Support

The relentless attacks we face as followers of God often signal that a breakthrough of divine favor is imminent. Satan's attempts to disrupt our lives target our commitment to daily Scripture study and the promises God has made to us and our families. He aims to divert our focus from the blessings God has prepared for us. Yet, with personal dedication and God's strength, we are called to manifest the potential He has placed within us. Just as a single good seed can yield a fruitful tree and a rich harvest, a single act of divine favor can unleash a multitude of blessings, affecting not just us but generations to come.

God often uses life's storms to break our stubborn wills and teach us humility and patience. He allows these challenges to draw us closer to Him and to refine our spirits.

Conversing with God

God encourages open dialogue, as stated in Isaiah 1:18, "Come now, let us reason together." We can bring our fears, doubts, weaknesses, failures, and victories before Him. When seeking the strength to continue our life's race—achieving success both spiritually and physically—we should ask God to fortify us. Through His strength, we can fulfill the expectations He has set for us without fear of the journey ahead.

God is aware of our trials long before they unfold. He calls us to approach Him with confidence and faith, trusting Him in all things. Prayer should always be steeped in faith, as Romans 12:12 reminds us to be "joyful in hope, patient in affliction, faithful in prayer." We are to find joy in all circumstances because we know that everything works together for the good of those who love God and are called according to His purpose.

We are instructed to enter God's presence with thanksgiving and praise as per Psalm 100:4: "Enter his gates with thanksgiving and his courts with praise; give thanks to him and praise his name." God deserves continual praise for guiding us through challenges and leading us to victory. Therefore, we must always express gratitude for His endless mercies and grace.

God is described as a friend who sticks closer than a brother, our Counselor, Comforter, and Healer. The Psalms reflect this, filled with prayers and hymns of God's people during times of affliction and victory. David's life, a testament to seeking God in all circumstances, shows us that victory is always within reach when we depend on the Lord.

The Essence of Prayer

When the disciples sought guidance on prayer, Jesus emphasized simplicity and sincerity over elaborate words. As seen in Matthew 6, our prayers should acknowledge God's precedence in every aspect of our lives. God values the faith behind our words more than the words themselves, moved by a believer's genuine faith that He rewards those who diligently seek Him.

The Bible is replete with examples of transformation through salvation offered by Jesus Christ. These individuals were not inherently special or deserving but were given grace freely, just as we are. Some had sinned greatly, yet the gift of salvation through Christ was extended to them without prejudice. Isaiah 55:7 promises, "He will abundantly pardon anyone who asks Him for forgiveness," affirming that redemption is available to all, regardless of past transgressions.

God's Transformative Power

God continues to transform lives across the globe, affecting people from every walk of life. He is the ultimate transformer, working from the inside out to produce inward changes that manifest outwardly as practical, godly living. If you have felt the call of the gospel of Jesus Christ in your heart but have not yet committed to follow Him, consider this your invitation. Now is the time to decide, while there is still time. Many of God's prayer warriors are interceding on your behalf, praying that you will see the light of Christ and submit your life to the authority of our loving, gracious, and merciful God. He is ready to undertake His incredible work of transformation in your life through His amazing grace and boundless love.

Examples of the Prayer of Faith

The Bible provides many inspiring examples of effective prayer. In 2 Chronicles 20, we learn about Jehoshaphat, the king of Judah, and his response to an impending attack by the Ammonites and Moabites. Faced with great fear, Jehoshaphat set himself to earnestly seek the Lord, proclaiming a fast throughout all of Judah. People from every city in Judah gathered to seek God's help.

Jehoshaphat stood before the congregation of Judah and prayed fervently. God responded through the prophet Jahaziel, assuring the people that they need not be dismayed by the multitude of their enemies because the battle was not theirs, but God's. He instructed them to stand still, in humility, and witness the salvation He would bring. God's message was clear: "Do not fear or be discouraged; the Lord is with you against your enemies." True to His word, Judah won the battle without fighting, for they trusted in God and praised Him for the victory. This brought peace throughout Judah, as the people celebrated and praised God for His deliverance.

Just as God delivered Jehoshaphat and the people of Judah, He is ready to do the same for us today. We must trust Him completely and allow Him to handle our battles, which are not only against external foes like persecution or adversity but also internal struggles such as illness, grief, depression, and financial hardship.

In 2 Chronicles 6, we read King Solomon's prayer when he dedicated the temple he built for God to live with His people. Solomon prayed for Israel and also for any foreigners who wanted the Lord. He asked God to live among His people and to pardon their sins, admitting their faults before God. Solomon's prayers were for God's presence to be shown in the temple, a holy place for God's glory, where all people could look for and praise Him.

So King Solomon urged the Almighty to enter His dwelling place, He and the ark of His power. And the King asked the Lord God to let those who serve Him be dressed with deliverance and make His faithful ones glad in His kindness. And the Bible tells us in 2 Chronicles 7:1–3, after King Solomon had finished his prayers to God, that fire descended from the sky and devoured the burnt offerings and the sacrifices. And the splendor of the Lord filled God's house.

If King Solomon could make a stone house for the Lord God to live in it with His people, and then give it to Him and praise Him with offerings and sacrifices, and God was pleased with those who praised Him and showed it by burning the offerings and sacrifices with fire, and God listened to King Solomon's prayer and forgave Israel for all their wrongdoings and filled the house with His glory, wouldn't God also listen to our prayers for the forgiveness of our wrongdoings?

Living in Faithful Dependence

These examples teach us the power of humble, faith-filled prayer. Whether facing overwhelming odds like Jehoshaphat or dedicating efforts to God's glory like Solomon, the key is complete dependence on God. By trusting in His might and submitting to His will, we can experience the profound impact of His intervention in our lives.

The truth that sets us free from the bondage of sin. When God sanctifies us, He cleanses us and makes us holy through His presence and His Word. As believers, our lives are temples of the Holy Spirit, where God's presence should manifest in every aspect of our behavior and interactions. By living in accordance to His Word and being vessels of His grace, we demonstrate to the world the transformative power of His love.

Dedication and Sanctification

Just as King Solomon dedicated the temple with sacrifices that pleased the Lord, we too are called to dedicate ourselves wholly to God. This dedication is not just symbolic but is evidenced through our daily lives and spiritual commitments. When Solomon's prayers were followed by divine signs—fire from heaven and the glory of the Lord filling the temple—it confirmed God's pleasure and presence.

In our modern context, while we may not see fire descend from the heavens,we witness God's presence through changes within us and the impact we make in the lives of others. Our offerings are no longer burnt sacrifices but the sacrifices of self—our time, efforts, and hearts committed to God's purposes. By crucifying our fleshly desires on the cross of humility and allowing God to fill us with His glory, we become living testimonies of His grace.

The Living Temple

Our bodies are temples of the Holy Spirit, meant not just for our personal sanctification but as beacons of light and hope to others. Just as the temple in Jerusalem was a place where both the faithful and the seekers could come to experience God, our lives should be open, inviting places where others can learn about and experience God's love and salvation.

By letting God consecrate us for His holy purposes, we embody the church He desires—a community of believers who not only worship Him in spirit and truth but also extend His kingdom through acts of love, mercy, and righteousness. This commitment helps bring those who do not yet know God into a relationship with Him, turning our spiritual journey into a collective experience that enriches our communities and the world.

Facing Life's Storms with Faith

God never promised an easy path; instead, He offered His presence as our guide through every storm and challenge. The tempests we face can either unmoor us or push us closer to Him, depending on our response. If we choose faith over fear, we not only endure but also grow stronger in our trust and reliance on Him.

Some storms will be hidden from everyone but you and God. Don't look at the storms to find Jesus. You can only know and feel His presence by faith, as He protects you from drowning in doubt and unbelief . And so God He is with you, in your fleshly vessel, His temple, in your storm.

As we navigate through life's uncertainties, let us hold fast to the promise that "we walk by faith, not by sight" (2 Corinthians 5:7). Our faith provokes the spiritual forces against us, but it also activates God's intervention in our lives for greater is God who is in us a than the adversary and enemy of our souls and peace who is in the world. God promises light after darkness, joy after sorrow, and peace after turmoil—blessings that come not despite our struggles but often because of them.

Conclusion

In summary, as we dedicate our lives as living temples to God for Him to dwell in us forever, let us remember His faithfulness and His promises for He is a covenant keeping God. He has never gone back on His Word and He never will. He is with us in every storm, ready to transform our trials into triumphs. Nothing in our experiences in this life, whether good or bad is wasted in the hands of an all-popwerful Creator God.

Through faith, let us come boldly before the throne of God, expecting His power to manifest in and through us as we commit to being His holy vessels. This is the joy of knowing Jesus, a joy far surpassing life without

Him. Trust in God's process, for if He leads you to it, He will indeed lead you through it, sanctifying you for His glory.

Who Jesus Is: Freedom from Satan's Grip

Knowing who Jesus is can liberate you and your family from Satan's control and tyranny. God will surround you and your loved ones with His presence, making it impossible for the enemy, who seeks to kill, steal, and destroy, to succeed.

In 1 Samuel 1, we read how Hannah, though barren because "the Lord had closed her womb," remained diligent and faithful in her prayers. God heard her and blessed her with a son, Samuel, who grew to be a mighty prophet in Israel.

Similarly, Acts 12 recounts how the early church prayed fervently for Peter's release from prison. God answered their prayers, sending an angel to free Peter, showcasing a miraculous deliverance through the power of collective prayer. In Ephesians 6 the Word of God says "And pray in the Spirit on all occasions with all kinds of prayers and requests. With this in mind, be alert and always keep on praying for all the Lord's people."

This teaches us an important lesson: if we pray in faith, on behalf of others, to be freed from their prisons—whether literal or figurative—God will respond. Our prayers could be for a family member, a coworker, a neighbor, our community, the government, or even a stranger. When our prayers are sincere, God will surely answer.

We should seek God in prayer for matters that align with His will, rather than for trivial, selfish desires. If we do, we will witness a divine movement in our lives, our communities, our neighborhoods, and across nations, unlike anything before. In Acts 16:25–26, during their darkest hour, Paul and Silas prayed and sang praises to God. Their faith shook the foundations of their prison, setting all captives free.

In times of unbearable trials, when God's hand seems absent, remember that He hears us (1 John 5:14-15). He can shake the very foundations of hell itself to free us from the bondage of sin and evil habits that tether us to Satan.

Trouble is temporary. "Weeping may stay for the night, but rejoicing comes in the morning" (Psalm 30:5). Ecclesiastes 3:1-8 reminds us that there is a time and season for everything under heaven. Just as nature cycles through seasons—trees shed leaves in autumn and bloom anew in spring—so too will God renew the parched areas of our lives. After storms,

He brings rainbows as signs of His covenant. And we know that "all things work together for good to those who love God" (Romans 8:28). Embrace every season of life, for each brings opportunities for learning and growth.

Let us be fervent and diligent in our prayers, trusting fully in God. Hebrews 4:9-12 invites us to enter into God's rest, ceasing from our works just as God did from His. The Word of God is alive and active, sharper than any double-edged sword, discerning the thoughts and attitudes of the heart. God is omniscient, aware of all our actions, both seen and unseen.

Therefore, we must go boldly to the throne of grace, asking God to guide us through His Word on how to live righteously beyond the veil of our flesh and in the spirit.

Transformation Through Trust in God

Knowing Jesus brings freedom from the grip of Satan, transforming our inner selves. If we truly believe and trust God to handle what we cannot, life becomes significantly easier, irrespective of external circumstances.

Prayer is a sacred time for God's children, characterized by reverence, humility, and honesty. God knows every detail of our lives, and no deceit can hide anything from Him. Many Christians suffer due to hidden aspects of their lives they refuse to surrender to God, causing unnecessary hardship.

The Bible, in Psalm 139:23-24, teaches us to invite God's scrutiny into our hearts and minds, asking Him to lead us on an everlasting path. Christians must open every aspect of their lives to God, allowing His complete restoration, so they may embody the likeness of Jesus in their daily lives. Jesus calls those burdened by life's cares to find rest in Him, fulfilling His purpose for coming into the world as the Lord Jesus Christ. From the moment sin entered humanity in Eden, causing a shift from peace to unrest, Christ became our refuge for total rest and deliverance from sin.

Our struggles with mental, emotional, and psychological pain could be alleviated if we listened to God, sought His counsel patiently, and followed His directions as outlined in Scripture. The scars of life often come from disobedience and impatience, deviating from God's commands. Just as parents set rules for their children's welfare, God's directives aim to guide us.

God, mighty and powerful, has already defeated the forces of evil through Christ's sacrifice on the cross. You must never believe that you are insignificant or unloved; God values you immensely, contradicting Satan's deceitful narrative that you are worthless. The Bible contrasts the devil's destructive intent with Christ's mission: to provide a full and abundant life (John 10:10). Reject the devil's lies, cling to hope, and never underestimate your worth in God's eyes.

At this moment, surrender entirely to God, who created you and seeks to renew your existence. Satan aims to destroy, but Christ offers a life of abundance. Let God instigate this transformation, and let Him make all things new in your life.

Let Christ reign in your life from today forward. He will return for a people living by every word from God, prepared for His imminent and glorious return. Be vigilant, maintain purity through obedience to God's Word, and you will be blessed (Revelation 16:15).

Prayer is essential for Christians, acting as a direct line to God and overcoming life's challenges. Many fail to recognize it as our most potent defense against the devil. Satan cannot comprehend the power of prayer, shielded by God's presence and unintelligible to his minions.

Overcoming Satan's Schemes Through Faithful Prayer

Satan's ultimate goal is to sever the connection between God's children and their Heavenly Father. He delights in seeing us complain and doubt God's promises, pushing us towards a life marked by defeat and misery. However, the prayers of a Christian—faithful and filled with genuine worship—are like incense to God, a sweet-smelling fragrance of true devotion.

Prayers driven by selfish motives or attempts to deceive God fail to enter His divine circuit, as anything tainted by sin is obliterated in His holy presence. Therefore, brothers and sisters, I urge you to earnestly seek God through prayer and immerse yourselves in His Word. This is how He will unveil His will for your life, guiding you away from the snares of the devil and towards a life of victorious faith.

CHAPTER 14

GOD'S WILL FOR YOUR LIFE

The Call to Sanctification Through Christ

Anyone who has accepted the Lord Jesus as their Savior is sanctified by the truth of God's Word. As Jesus declared in John 17:17, "Sanctify them through thy truth: thy word is truth." Sanctification involves being set apart for God's exclusive use, embodying holiness, which in Greek (hagiasmos) means precisely that—"to make holy." This process demands self-denial, total surrender, and reliance on God, countering our innate desire to manage life independently and often destructively.

The Greek word translated sanctification (hagiasmos) means "holiness."18 To sanctify, therefore, means "to make holy." This is a process of self-denial, total surrender, and dependence upon God. The nature of humanity is to "do-it-yourself." And it is that "do-it-yourself" nature that always wants to be in charge and get things done its own way. Thus, we live our lives in self-destructive ways. And it is only God who can help us detangle out from the mess we put ourselves in because of mankind's stubbornness not to live life God's way.

Many people, even some who say that they know God, try to use Him on an as-needed basis like they use other people. But God cannot be used by anyone. And so by nature, all mankind would rather keep God out of their lives when things appear to be well with them. Some people try to fit Him in, only if they believe He exists anyway, when they are in serious trouble with Satan on their heels, and all hell is breaking loose in their lives. The true children will God to lead in their lives His way, no matter what cost they may have to endure. And so if Jesus Christ is our Lord, wherefore, He is leading the way in our lives, then we ought to obey all His commandments (1 John 2 and 5).

18Storng's Greek # 38.

Sanctification is a divine act where God, through His Word, extricates worldly influences from His redeemed children. It contrasts with salvation—the power of Jesus' blood to remove those who respond to God's call from worldly entanglements.

Unfortunately, many, including some who profess to know God, treat Him as a mere convenience, akin to how they might use others—only recognizing His existence in times of dire need, when Satan's threats loom large, and chaos ensues. This approach to faith does not align with God's desire for a complete relationship with us. God engages with our whole being and is not satisfied with lukewarm or inconsistent commitment. He calls for our entirety, either to transform us from spiritual coldness into fervor or reject our half-hearted attempts altogether.

God does not guide those who waver in their commitment. Deliberately withholding aspects of our lives from Him limits His ability to intervene beneficially. Christians who have restricted God's access to certain rebellious parts of their lives have faced severe consequences. We cannot simultaneously serve God and the world; a decision is required, and any compromise is essentially a victory for Satan.

God aims to break our stubborn will to reshape us, creating a new heart and a right spirit within, integrating us perfectly with Jesus, the divine vine. Many resist this transformation, feeling overwhelmed by God's commands and fearing loss of control over their lives. Yet, the path to a holy and sanctified life necessarily involves crucifying our selfish desires.

Life remains arduous until we humble ourselves—or are humbled by God—to recognize His sovereignty. True Christians let God's will lead, regardless of the personal cost, fulfilling the call to obey all His commandments, as outlined in 1 John chapters 2 and 5.

Success God's Way

The world's definition of success often emphasizes power, prestige, position, educational accomplishments, and wealth. This societal view measures success by the car one drives, the house one lives in, and the size of one's net worth. However, if these tangible assets are the sole indicators of success, then we are equating the value of life to merely perishable earthly items.

As a society, it is a grave error to set both ourselves and our children up for failure by using material possessions and secular values as yardsticks for success and human worth. Instead, God calls His followers to adopt the Bible's standard of success, which promises fulfillment in every aspect of our lives. True success, according to divine guidance, involves listening to and acting upon God's Word. Living a godly life invariably leads one in the right direction.

We ought to gauge a person's worth by the content of their character, the true gold standard of . Only God truly understands what success entails. He instructs us to seek first His kingdom and His righteousness, with the assurance that everything else will follow. The kingdom of God, as described in Romans 14:17, comprises righteousness, peace, and joy in the Holy Spirit. It is the inner treasure of godliness that truly matters.

A life devoid of a relationship with God might seem successful, but it's susceptible to collapse under life's trials. When faced with hardships that strip away our material possessions, those who rely solely on such assets find themselves unanchored. However, those who anchor their lives in God lose nothing of real value; God is capable of restoring and even enhancing our lives with blessings that glorify Him.

Consider Job's unwavering faith and his profound relationship with God. Despite severe trials, he was ultimately blessed doubly, exemplifying that with God, we lack nothing. Our true worth is determined by God's love for humanity, demonstrated through the sacrifice of His Son, Jesus Christ, ensuring eternal life for believers.

God's definition of success transcends the mere accumulation of wealth. It involves obedience to His Word and developing a character that glorifies God and serves others. Only God can foster such godly character within us.

God must be the priority in every believer's life. He is above all earthly concerns. While God desires for His people to thrive in all areas, true prosperity and success must be nurtured in fertile spiritual soil—a heart receptive to God's Word and a life that bears the fruit of the Spirit. Attributes such as truth, honesty, integrity, mercy, goodness, purity, faithfulness, gentleness, long-suffering, peace, and joy are the marks of a true child of God and the keys to genuine success.

As bearers of Christ, we become fertile ground for His Word, allowing us to yield abundant spiritual fruit. Conversely, without Christ, one risks harboring seeds of mischief as enumerated in Galatians 5, including adultery, idolatry, hatred, and strife, among others. Ultimately, the choice of path influences the nature of success one achieves.

Living Beyond Material Needs: Spiritual Nourishment from God's Word

Luke 4:4 emphasizes, "It is written, That man shall not live by bread alone, but by every word of God." This passage underscores the contrast between the tangible necessities of life, such as bread, and the spiritual nourishment provided by God's Word. While material sustenance is essential, it pales in comparison to the enduring peace and wisdom that come from prioritizing the kingdom of God. If one's life revolves solely around earthly needs without embracing the living Word of God, enduring peace through life's storms remains elusive. Material possessions can facilitate comfort, but they are incapable of providing the profound, lasting peace and joy that only comes from God.

God's Word not only nourishes but also offers counsel and encouragement, guiding us through life's challenges. The transient nature of worldly kingdoms is starkly contrasted with the eternal nature of God's kingdom, which holds the everlasting treasures bestowed upon us. This connection between our heart and our treasure is pivotal, as highlighted by the assertion that our hearts will always align with what we value most.

The wisdom of the world often falls short, providing inadequate solutions to life's complexities. In contrast, divine wisdom is limitless, equipping God's children with everything necessary to navigate life effectively. The Word of God is described as a seed that continually grows within believers, bearing good fruit and flourishing like a spring of living water sourced from Jesus Christ. Those nourished by this water will not thirst for worldly things, and their deeds of righteousness will thrive under God's watchful presence.

Joshua 1 offers a powerful illustration of this principle. God instructed Joshua to adhere strictly to His Word, promising that such obedience would lead to prosperity and success. This divine directive was clear: meditate on and follow God's law without deviation, ensuring both prosperity and righteous success.

Thus, true success is not costly but rather the natural outcome of obedience to God's commands. Conversely, the price of disobedience is high, leading to a type of success that sacrifices a clear conscience and the development of a godly character. God's teachings also guide us to sacrifice our carnal desires, allowing Him to refine us into new creations aligned with His divine intentions.

Jesus's invitation in Matthew 11:28–30 reassures us that following Him is not burdensome but liberating. His yoke is light, freeing us from the weight of sin and leading us toward restful souls, demonstrating that God's paths, unlike worldly burdens, are meant to be uplifting and freeing.

The Role of God's Law in Christian Life

Some Christians argue that because Christ redeemed us from the curse of the law, we are no longer required to keep the law of God. However, Galatians 3:13 clarifies this misconception: Christ redeemed us from the curse of the law by becoming the curse for us. This redemption does not invalidate the law but frees us from the penalty it imposes for disobedience. The law itself identifies sin and administers a curse for its transgression. When we live by God's Word, we are following the path that Christ set for us—doing what He commands and refraining from what He forbids. This obedience is not merely legalistic adherence but a manifestation of the love that God instills in His children, enabling them to lead pure and consecrated lives, serving as godly examples for others.

The law does not justify; it is God who justifies (Romans 8:33). The law serves as a guide to Jesus Christ, the true source of salvation, by defining sin and revealing God's perfect, holy, and righteous nature. It points sinners to Christ, our advocate, rather than acting as a means of salvation. Only through Christ's sacrifice can we be redeemed from our sins (Romans 3:20, Psalm 19:7).

Galatians 3:27 states, "For as many of you as have been baptized into Christ have put on Christ." This transformative experience means that in our reborn spirits, we possess the character of God. Jesus taught that love for Him is demonstrated through obedience to His commandments (John 14:15). Thus, if we are not engaging in sin—murder, idolatry, falsehood, or immorality—we are not under the law's condemnation but under Christ's grace, empowered by Him to live righteously.

Those who claim it is impossible to keep God's law are correct in one sense—it is impossible outside of Christ. Yet, within Christ, keeping the law is synonymous with living according to God's Word. Commands like loving God and our neighbors, or refraining from theft, are inherent in the law and integral to our Christ-like nature. This new nature fosters a genuine desire to fulfill God's will, drawing us from darkness into His marvelous light.

God's commandments are not burdensome; they are lighter than the worldly burdens we once bore. A life aligned with God's Word naturally avoids willful sin. Why then should we not relinquish the heavy burdens of life to God? These burdens lead to depression and loneliness, depriving us of God's richest blessings.

Jesus's words in Matthew 6:24-34 reinforce that no one can serve two masters. We cannot oscillate between serving God and indulging in sin. Living in the flesh with its sinful desires while attempting to be a doer of the Word is fundamentally impossible, for the two are in direct opposition.

We must recognize that compromising our integrity for fleeting gains only leads to empty results. God, in His nature, never compromises on righteousness and does not condone sin. We must be grateful for God's grace and mercy, which sustain us even as we struggle with sin, and thank Him for sparing us from the dire consequences of our actions.

The Holiness of God and His Expectations for Us

God embodies holiness, justice, and righteousness. He is incapable of sin and sets a divine standard for His children to aspire to—holiness, justice, and righteousness. Unlike God, humans are born into sin and shaped by iniquity (Psalm 51:5), predisposed to err due to our fallen nature. God, pure and untainted, neither tempts nor can be tempted by evil (James 1:13). Instead, human sinfulness is driven by fleshly desires and Satanic temptations.

In Matthew 6, Jesus instructs us not to worry about our basic needs—what to eat, drink, or wear. Worry clouds our minds with doubt and disrupts our ability to engage with God's Word effectively. Anxiety sends our brains into a fight-or-flight response, leading to irrational decisions and vulnerability to sin. Satan exploits this confusion, preying on our weakened state. Hence, worrying not only fails to resolve our concerns but often exacerbates them, leading us away from relying on God's wisdom.

God alone can meet our needs at the precise moment they need to be addressed. His omniscience assures us that He is fully aware of our needs and capable of providing for them. As children of God, our primary responsibility is to trust Him completely, seek His Kingdom and His righteousness, and believe that He will take care of our material needs accordingly.

Who God Is to Us

Our perception of God should be grounded in the Scriptures and the insights we receive from the Holy Spirit. The Bible illustrates that God is deeply involved in every aspect of our lives. Jesus proclaimed, "I am come that they might have life, and that they might have it more abundantly" (John 10:10), signifying His intent to cleanse and renew every part of our existence. Jesus's mission was to seek and save the lost (Luke 19:10), offering redemption and transformation to all who respond to His call.

God is far from being an aloof celestial being; He is intimately acquainted with the complexities of human life. He wants His children to collaborate with Him in achieving their God-given potential and success. God did not create us to be passive observers but active participants in a productive and meaningful life. You are immensely valuable to God—so much so that He was willing to sacrifice His glory and take on sin to provide a path of salvation. If there had been only one sinner, Christ would have still come to save that individual, demonstrating the infinite worth of every soul to God.

God's commitment to us is unwavering; it is we who often forget or turn away from Him. Understanding our value to God and His expectations for us should inspire a life of obedience, service, and profound trust in His providential care.

God's Unforgettable Love and the Path to Purification

Isaiah 49:15-16 offers a profound reminder of God's unwavering commitment to His people: "Can a woman forget her sucking child, that she should not have compassion on the son of her womb? Yes, they may forget, yet I will not forget thee. Behold, I have graven thee upon the palms of My hands." This passage reassures us that God's memory of us is indelible, and His care is constant.

God's justice and righteousness ensure that His demands are fair—He never expects from us what is beyond our capability. However, He does call us to engage daily with His Word, which is crucial for cleansing our minds from iniquity and the remnants of sin. Through regular meditation on Scripture, we cultivate thoughts that align with purity and holiness, empowering us to resist satanic temptations and the urges of our flesh.

Transformed by God Alone!

The Bible shapes our thinking, acting as a shield guarding our minds from evil influences and fostering righteous living. The principle is clear: by storing God's Word in our hearts, we prevent sin from taking root. This practice is not merely about avoidance but is a proactive stride toward godly living.

As we immerse ourselves in Scripture, our minds are renewed by the power of God's Word, allowing us to manifest the fruits of the Spirit in our lives. In Christ, we are new creations, incapable of navigating this world's complexities without divine guidance. Without God's direction, we are prone to wander into confusion and chaos.

God's refining process often involves allowing us to endure uncomfortable situations to mold us into Christ's image. This is not punishment but purification, designed to transform us into the precious jewels He intends us to be. Through trials, often described as a fiery furnace of affliction, God does not abandon us but accompanies us, controlling the furnace's heat and protecting us from its potential harm.

1 Peter 4:12 counsels us not to be bewildered by fiery trials, as these are not unusual but integral to our spiritual growth and endurance. God uses these challenges to refine our character, enhancing our reliance on Him and deepening our faith.

Enduring Trials with Christ as Our Guide

In Isaiah 49:15-16, God reassures us that, unlike a mother who might forget her child, He will never forget His people, symbolically engraving them on the palms of His hands. This powerful imagery underlines God's unwavering commitment to His children throughout all circumstances, including trials and tribulations.

As Christians, we encounter various trials, not as punishments, but as tests of faith that refine our character and strengthen our dependence on God. 1 Peter 4:12-13 reminds us not to be surprised by these fiery trials, for they are part of sharing in Christ's sufferings. When we endure these hardships, we are invited to rejoice because we are being prepared to partake in Christ's glory.

Sanctification is an ongoing journey that begins the moment we are cleansed from sin by Christ. It involves daily growth in righteousness, aided by the Holy Spirit, and will culminate gloriously at Christ's return when our mortal bodies will be transformed into immortality.

Christ's own trials, temptations, and sufferings, which He overcame, provide us with a blueprint for victory. As His followers, we are not merely to endure but to conquer with the assurance that Jesus has already secured our triumph. This victory is not just theoretical but practical, requiring obedience to Christ's teachings and a deep trust in Him to navigate us through life's challenges.

You are purchased at a price—the life of Jesus Christ. His sacrifice grants us freedom from the eternal consequences of sin and calls us into a life of submission to His lordship. Luke 6:46 challenges us to align our actions with our declarations of Jesus as Lord, embracing a lifestyle that reflects His teachings and purity.

Walking in the Footsteps of Christ

Following Jesus requires self-denial and taking up our cross daily, as stated in Matthew 16:24. This path is not about solitary suffering; it involves walking in the footsteps that Christ Himself has set before us. The psalmist assures us in Psalms 37:23 that the steps of a righteous man are ordered by the Lord, delighting in His way. Thus, every step we take under His guidance brings us closer to the person God intends us to become.

Christ's way is perfect and leads us away from the snares of the flesh and the devil. As followers, our eyes must remain fixed on Jesus, especially during the storms of life. When chaos ensues, like Christ who calmed the sea, we too can find peace in the assurance that He commands even the elements.

As vessels destined for holiness, we are called to be zealous for good works (Titus 2:14), reflecting God's purity in everything we do. Our lives should exemplify the transformation Christ brings, helping others to know Him as their Savior and Lord. By living out the potential Christ has unlocked for us, we can guide others toward the same transformative experience.

Honoring God with Our Bodies: Diet and Dress

As followers of Christ, we must recognize that our bodies are temples of the Holy Spirit, entrusted to us by God (1 Corinthians 6:19-20). We are called to honor God by maintaining our physical health through conscientious living, which includes mindful eating and dressing.

Biblical Principles for Healthy Eating

God has outlined a specific diet in the Scriptures, promoting a diet rich in fruits, vegetables, and nuts—the diet originally given in the Garden of Eden. Leviticus 11 details the consumption of 'clean meats,' emphasizing that these should not contain blood. Adhering to these dietary guidelines not only aligns us with God's instructions but also brings significant health benefits, as many Christians can attest.

Many illnesses are exacerbated or directly caused by poor dietary choices. By adopting the diet God has prescribed, we can prevent or even reverse many of these conditions, fulfilling God's desire for His people to enjoy robust mental and physical health (3 John 2). When we struggle with making these healthy choices, Christ stands ready to strengthen our faith and assist us in overcoming harmful habits.

Christian Modesty: Health and Witness through Apparel

Modesty in dress is a testimony of our commitment to God. Our clothing choices should not impede physical health, such as by restricting blood circulation or impairing the skin's ability to regulate body temperature. Tight, restrictive clothing can lead to a variety of health issues. While Scripture does not dictate specific apparel, it encourages us to consider whether our dress glorifies God or ourselves.

It is crucial to approach fashion with a mindset that respects our bodies as temples of the Holy Spirit. The Bible challenges us to focus on humility and obedience rather than external appearances. In churches and community settings, our choice of attire should support the spiritual growth of others, not cause stumbling due to inappropriateness or ostentation.

Additionally, the choice of footwear, particularly for women, deserves attention. High heels and other fashionable shoes can cause long-term musculoskeletal problems. As we age, the toll of such choices becomes evident. Balancing attractiveness with practicality and comfort is essential to avoid future health complications.

Living the Gospel: Health, Holiness, and Witness

John's third epistle expresses a deep wish for the health and prosperity of God's children, emphasizing the need for harmony between the mind and body. This holistic health is essential for Christians not only for personal well-being but also for effective ministry.

Effective Witnessing Through Personal Transformation

Visibility of God's work in our lives serves as a powerful testament to the transformative power of the Gospel. If we live out the teachings of Jesus authentically, people are more likely to be drawn to the message we share. The manner in which we maintain our health, manage our thoughts, and dress ourselves speaks volumes about the change God has wrought in us. This alignment of thought and action is critical, as Proverbs 23:7 reminds us that we become what we think. If our minds are filled with divine thoughts, our lives will reflect God's holiness.

To truly reflect Christ, we must consecrate ourselves to God's purposes, embracing and embodying the righteousness of Christ. This transformation necessitates purging ungodly behaviors and thoughts, as a Christian's life is a mirror of their true spiritual state. Actions that contradict the teachings of Christ might indicate a lack of genuine conversion.

Purification Through Trials and Spiritual Disciplines

God often uses trials to cleanse us, preparing us to be vessels of His grace. If there are areas in our lives displeasing to Him, it is these very issues God targets to refine us. Embracing these corrections can remove barriers to receiving God's blessings, including eternal life promised in 2 Corinthians 4:4, which states that Satan blinds the minds of unbelievers.

Additionally, the practice of fasting, as described in Isaiah 58:6–7, is not merely abstaining from food but engaging in acts of justice and mercy. This type of fasting challenges us to break the bonds of wickedness, relieve burdens, and actively care for those in need. It's a spiritual discipline that transforms us, making our character more Christ-like.

The Real Measure of Our Love for God

Our love for God is measured by how we treat those around us. It is contradictory to claim love for God while harboring malice or engaging in deceit towards others. True Christian love extends beyond mere words to sacrificial action and genuine interpersonal relations.

This call to live out the Gospel comprehensively includes how we care for our bodies, interact with others, and face spiritual challenges. As believers, our actions must consistently reflect the teachings of Christ, showing that we are His disciples not just in word, but in deed.

Holistic Health and Spiritual Integrity in Christian Life
Holistic Health as a Testament to Faith

In 3 John 2, we are reminded, "Beloved, I wish above all things that thou mayest prosper and be in health, even as thy soul prospereth." This scripture underscores the importance of harmony between mental, physical, and spiritual health, affirming that God's desire for us extends to all facets of well-being. As the temple of God, regular exercise, adequate rest, and a healthy diet are not just physical necessities but spiritual obligations. By caring for our bodies, we enhance our capacity to serve God effectively and become competent witnesses for Christ.

Living the Gospel Authentically

Visibility in our transformation is a powerful witness to the truth of the Gospel. When others observe us embodying the teachings of Jesus, particularly in how we manage our health and thoughts, they are more likely to be drawn to His message. Proverbs 23:7 teaches, "As a man thinketh in his heart, so is he," highlighting the profound impact of our thoughts on our actions. By nurturing godly thoughts and rejecting wicked ones, we manifest Christ in our lives, encouraging others to seek Him.

Purification Through Discipline and Trials

Our journey with Christ involves continuous self-examination and purification, as true discipleship demands a life free from sin's stronghold. This purification process often involves trials and spiritual disciplines like fasting and prayer, which refine our character and align us more closely with God's will. Isaiah 58:6-7 outlines the fast God chooses—one focused on justice, mercy, and humility. This type of fasting involves active engagement in relieving oppression and addressing needs within the community, which in turn fosters personal spiritual growth and societal transformation.

Consistency in Christian Love

The authenticity of our love for God is measured by our actions towards others. It is contradictory to profess love for God while harboring hatred or malice towards anyone, as articulated in 1 John 3:18, "Let us not love with words or speech but with actions and in truth." Our interactions with family, friends, and strangers should reflect the love and kindness that Christ taught, without bias or hypocrisy.

Living Out Our Faith

We must earnestly seek God's guidance in every aspect of our lives, ensuring our actions do not contradict our faith. This includes maintaining a lifestyle that is not only healthy but also morally and spiritually sound. We are called to not only hear God's Word but to implement it diligently, allowing it to transform us into the image of Christ.

By embracing these principles, we not only live healthier, more fulfilled lives but also become beacons of God's love and truth in a world in need of His grace.

Self-Denial and Self-Sacrifice in Christian Life

The Apostle Paul in Romans 12 calls every believer to present their bodies as a living sacrifice, holy and pleasing to God—this is the true and proper worship. As new creations in Christ, we are not defined by denominational lines or doctrinal interpretations but by our personal transformation through Christ alone. This transformation involves a total surrender to God's will, allowing His Spirit to renew our minds and change our hearts as we study, meditate, and embody His Word.

Transformation Through Christ

The path to sanctification is not through human effort or adherence to external religious standards but through a deep, personal relationship with Jesus Christ. 2 Corinthians 5:17 emphasizes, "Therefore, if anyone is in Christ, the new creation has come: The old has gone, the new is here!" This transformation breaks the chains of sin and ushers us into a life of freedom, as promised in John 8:36, "So if the Son sets you free, you will be free indeed."

The Daily Struggle and Victory

Despite being redeemed, Christians still face a daily struggle between the desires of the flesh and the spirit. The flesh may lead us towards sin, but our reborn spirit, infused by God, strives for obedience to His commandments. The apostle Paul describes this conflict in 1 Corinthians 2:14, noting that "the person without the Spirit does not accept the things that come from the Spirit of God but considers them foolishness." Thus, we are called to die daily to sin and live according to the Spirit, which bears good fruit and glorifies God.

Lessons from Jacob's Transformation

Jacob's transformation, as described in Genesis 32:24-29, serves as a profound illustration of wrestling with God and emerging changed. Jacob, originally a schemer, encountered God and wrestled with Him until dawn. This pivotal moment led to his renaming as Israel, signifying his struggle with God and with humans and overcoming. This story not only symbolizes the struggle but also the divine change that can occur when one truly encounters God. Jacob's physical limp served as a lifelong reminder of his dependence on God's strength, teaching us that our weaknesses are perfected in His power.

Living the Transformed Life

As believers, our lives should reflect this constant leaning on and learning from God. Every aspect of our existence, from our thoughts to our actions, is visible to God, and we must strive to align them with His will. The challenge to live in self-denial and sacrifice is not about losing ourselves but about finding our true purpose and joy in God.

In embracing these principles, we not only adhere to the biblical call of sanctification but also enable ourselves to live out a faith that is dynamic, transformative, and a true witness to the power of Christ in our lives.

Divine Transformation: God's Work Within Us

True transformation can only be achieved through the divine intervention of God. No human effort or self-help program can fully change a person from the inside out; only God's power can bring about a complete and lasting change. Romans 12:1-2 instructs believers to present their bodies as living sacrifices, holy and pleasing to God, which is our true and proper worship. This transformation involves a renewal of the mind—a process that transcends human philosophies and is solely the work of God.

Obedience Over Ritual

In the pursuit of holiness, it is not rituals or adherence to denominational doctrines that sanctify us, but our obedience to God's Word. God values this obedience far above the sacrifices that stem from mere ritualism or cultural conformity. True obedience involves a heart posture that is aligned with God's desires and commands, not just external compliance.

God's call to obedience is a call to abandon our own ways and fully embrace His will. This can be challenging, especially when what is taught by churches or denominations conflicts with the biblical truth. Therefore, everything we hear and practice should be tested against the Scripture, ensuring that our faith and conduct are grounded in what God has truly said.

God's Interest in Us

God is not interested in our material possessions or our philosophical ideas; He is the Creator of all and the master of the universe and beyond. His primary interest is in us—His creation—and in transforming us into His image. As stated in Romans 12, our transformation is God's desire for us to prove what is His good, acceptable, and perfect will.

The Call to Holiness and Service

God desires for His children to be holy, reflecting His character in all aspects of life. This call to holiness extends beyond personal purity to include active service to others. God equips us to meet both the spiritual and physical needs of those around us, turning our lives into a fragrant offering that is pleasing to Him.

Sustained by God in Trials

God promises to be with us through all seasons—whether in sickness or health, in prosperity or poverty. His commitment to us is unchanging and secured by His own oath. This assurance is our foundation when facing life's challenges, reminding us that we are never forsaken, regardless of our circumstances.

The Ultimate Purpose

Ultimately, God's work in us is not just about making us better for our own sake but preparing us to be vessels for His service. It is through our transformed lives that others can see the truth of the gospel—lives marked by godliness, kindness, and justice. God calls each believer to be a beacon of His light and love, embodying the change that He alone can bring about.

God's call is clear: He beckons us to come and be transformed, to lay down our old selves and take up a new identity in Him. Through this transformation, we are not only recipients of His eternal blessings but also participants in His divine mission.

Marriage Is an Act of Self-denial

Some marriages are centered around "me." In these relationships, both partners often withhold from each other the care and affection that, according to Biblical commands, should be generously shared. This sharing should be consistent unless mutually agreed upon interruptions occur, such as during times of fasting, prayer, or illness. The Bible emphasizes that husbands and wives should always support one another warmly. After any temporary pause, they must reunite to avoid temptations that could be exploited by Satan (1 Corinthians 7:1–5). Under no circumstances, barring health issues, should couples avoid each other as a form of punishment over trivial disagreements.

Using affection as a weapon in marital conflicts is sinful. The Scriptures instruct us to be honest and loving towards each other (Ephesians 4:25 and Zechariah 8:16). Failing to do so emulates behavior that Christ would never show towards His church. God sees through our excuses for being unaffectionate, recognizing such actions as deceitful. Such behavior is termed as defrauding one another in the Bible.

When spouses isolate themselves due to stubbornness or anger, it provides an opportunity for Satan to lead them into temptation. Many marriages sour due to selfishness and unwillingness to submit to God's will. Often, unresolved personal issues and unconfessed sins underlie this bitterness, hindering God's ability to mend our brokenness and improve our lives.

As Christians, we must place complete trust in God regarding our marriages. He is our truest friend and helper. Life need not be difficult with God as our counselor—He is just a prayer away from guiding us through our troubles, which invariably affect our marital relationships. However, refusing to seek His assistance ensures a challenging life filled with misery.

Spiritual dryness leads to discontent, affecting our homes and personal interactions. No Christian should harbor bitterness and anger. By inviting Christ into our lives, His transformative power can turn a chaotic, miserable marriage into one of peace and rest.

If we deny or ignore the promptings of the Holy Spirit to confess and repent, we block God's healing of our personal and marital issues. Without Christ's presence, we cannot find internal peace or enjoy a harmonious marriage. Unaddressed, our personal "baggage" delights

Satan, who thrives on our misery. Our unresolved issues not only torment us but also disrupt our marriages and family life.

We must surrender all ungodly aspects of our lives to God, placing them on the altar of sacrifice, no matter how shameful or painful. God, who spared nothing to redeem us—even death on the cross—desires to resurrect us from destructive habits and dead works. Sin must not govern our lives, marriages, or homes. Unconfessed sins pave the way for failure. A home filled with strife cannot flourish, and such an environment strains the marriage. Instead, enrich your life and marriage with the transformative power of God's Word. Surrender completely to Him, and He will imbue your life with the power to live victoriously, enriching your spirit and blessing your marriage.

Peaceful, happy marriages are possible when we are at peace with God, ourselves, and each other. This peace is attainable only through Jesus, for He alone can offer true rest (Matthew 11:28). It deeply grieves God to witness His followers acting selfishly and hatefully towards one another.

Every household will face the repercussions of living in defiance of God. Those engaging in sinful acts will face judgment for ignoring His commandments. Therefore, we must commit everything to God, allowing Him to transform us into better individuals, thus improving our marriages and making our homes more harmonious.

God's Patience and Our Responsibility

God is long-suffering, having granted us numerous opportunities to repent. He utilizes all resources at His disposal to cleanse us and our homes from sinful habits. If you feel that situations in your marriage or home have deteriorated beyond repair, remember that nothing is beyond God's capacity for restoration. He is the Almighty, capable of achieving the impossible. What we need to do is surrender our struggles to God and trust Him to liberate our marriages from the enemy's influence.

As husbands and wives, we must be mindful of how we treat each other. Our interactions often reflect the strength of our relationship with God. Christ taught that the greatest commandment is to love God with all our heart, soul, and mind. The second is to love our neighbors as ourselves (Matthew 22:37-39).

True love for God compels us to adhere to His Word, prompting couples to maintain their affection for each other regardless of life's challenges. Love should not be conditional, reserved only for when others treat us well. Instead, we should sustain our love even when facing difficulties, embodying the unconditional love that God shows us.

In the Bible, a 'neighbor' is defined as a friend, not an enemy. This love extends to both strangers and those close to us (Luke 10:25–36; Matthew 25:34–40). Therefore, our spouse is also our 'neighbor'—our friend, not our adversary, if we truly follow Christ. This book's perspective on marriage, as ordained in the Bible, is exclusively between a man and a woman.

We are instructed never to let the sun set on our anger, lest we become susceptible to Satan's temptations and sin (Ephesians 4:26). The ability to forgive genuinely is crucial so that God, in turn, can forgive us. It doesn't matter who is right or wrong; the imperative is to forgive as commanded by God. By setting aside pride and embodying the fruits of love, we shut out opportunities for Satan to lead us into sin. Worship in our marriages is essential. God doesn't just desire our marriages to survive; He wants them to thrive under His sovereign rule.

Both partners must remain vigilant about maintaining the spiritual and physical health of their marriage and home. Regular engagement with Scripture provides divine wisdom through the Holy Spirit. Addressing issues promptly and focusing on Jesus can help avert marital crises. It is vital for couples to be aware of their thoughts, ensuring that past hurts or sinful inclinations do not undermine their relationship or home. Husbands and wives must guard against the devil's schemes by fostering a robust and godly union.

Divine Healing and Love in Marriage

Nothing is too difficult for God to repair. He is capable of mending even what seems impossibly broken. The answers to our troubled marriages and broken hearts are not found in secular courts or through the advice of those with worldly perspectives.

True and lasting solutions emerge from the divine counsel—when we immerse ourselves in God's Word and seek Him in prayer for every personal anguish and marital discord. If we claim that God has transformed us, this change should be evident in how we treat each other. As God loves us unconditionally, so must we love one another without conditions. Husbands and wives are called to sacrifice their own desires, submitting their wills to God. By doing this, we close the doors to the opportunities Satan seeks to incite sin against God and each other.

Our relationship with God should transcend our feelings; it must be reflected in our daily lives. Loving God is a divine gift, as is the spirit of love He instills in us towards each other. This gift aims to foster our obedience, which in turn brings victory in our spiritual battles. Embracing the mind of Christ means undergoing a transformation from carnal impulses to a life centered on spiritual truth and sobriety.

A life consecrated to God worships in spirit and truth. Christ-like love is not driven by mere emotion; it is inherently kind and patient. It does not envy or boast. It is not proud or rude. True love is not self-seeking or easily angered; it keeps no record of wrongs. It does not delight in evil but rejoices with the truth. It always protects, always trusts, always hopes, always perseveres (1 Corinthians 13:4–7). This is the model of love our marriages should emulate, reflecting Christ's love for His church, with whom He is united as a groom to his bride. We must live as continual sacrifices to God, dying daily to sin so that we may be whole and pleasing to Him.

CHAPTER 15
God's Love and His Gift

The True Essence of Jesus Christ and His Ministry

Jesus Christ, known as Emmanuel, which means "God with us", never pursued earthly glory or notoriety during His ministry. He came into His own creation not to establish an earthly kingdom or government but to serve and give His life as a sacrifice. Jesus, who was in the form of God, did not consider equality with God as something to exploit but humbled Himself by taking on human form and becoming obedient to death on a cross (Philippians 2:6–8). He fully embraced humanity's sufferings and emotions, serving as our High Priest who is intimately acquainted with our weaknesses and yet without sin (Hebrews 4).

Christ's mission was not only to demonstrate what a relationship with God looks like but also to atone for humanity as the faultless Lamb of God, who takes away the sins of the world. Despite setting aside His divine privileges, He remained fully divine, the great I Am, Lord of lords and King of kings.

During His earthly life, Christ's humble appearance and the profound truths He proclaimed often led to misunderstanding and hatred from those around Him. Despite being without sin, He was despised for exposing the sins of humanity. He was crucified not for His own sins—since He committed none—but for ours, fulfilling the prophecies of being wounded for our transgressions and bruised for our iniquities (Isaiah 53:5).

God demonstrated His love for us by sending His Son to die for us while we were still sinners (Romans 5:8). This act of divine love offers salvation freely to anyone who asks, reflecting the undeserved favor of God. Christ's sacrifice on Calvary paid the ultimate price for our redemption, offering eternal life to all who believe by faith. This redemption was so profound that it secured our freedom from sin's bondage and rendered Satan's attempts at imitation futile.

Satan, characterized by deceit and destruction, lacks the capacity for love and cannot replicate the redemptive work of Christ. This truth emphasizes that our salvation is a gift from God, not earned by human deeds but by divine grace alone (Ephesians 2:8–9). God's passion through Christ extends beyond saving us; it aims to annihilate every influence of Satan in the lives of the redeemed.

Knowing you are wholly liberated through salvation should empower you to live confidently in the freedom Christ has secured. His grace satisfies God's justice, demanded by our sins, and extends mercy to prevent eternal damnation. As we surrender to His will, God's grace transforms us, fulfilling His righteous demands and enveloping us in His endless mercy and love.

The Dynamics of Grace in Overcoming Sin

God is merciful and offers endless opportunities for repentance. Those who humble themselves and acknowledge Him are cleansed from their sins and enabled to live and reign with Christ eternally.

Every believer enveloped in Christ's righteousness is purified from every sin through His blood, liberated from the wages of sin, and graced with divine peace. As recipients of God's profound love and partakers of His heavenly gift, believers are freed from the bondage of sin and Satan through God's grace.

Nevertheless, this grace should not be mistaken for a license to sin. Returning to sinful habits after Christ has canceled our debt is often a sign that the seed of God's Word was snatched away by Satan, who plants seeds of discouragement and doubt. The persistence of sin in some lives might also indicate that the word-seed fell on stony ground—the stubborn, unyielding human will that resists transformation and is choked by worldly cares.

True believers must not only hear God's Word but also become doers of it. When the redeemed act righteously, they provide tangible evidence of their faith (James 1:22). Demonstrating God's teachings through actions is essential in expressing our love for Him.

Jesus Christ, the perfect sacrificial Lamb, was slain to offer salvation to all who listen to the Holy Spirit and do not harden their hearts. Those who embrace this salvation will avoid the second death, which is the eternal destruction of both soul and body in the lake of fire. According to Ephesians 2, we were spiritually dead in our sins until God made us alive again in Christ. Originally connected to God, humanity lost spiritual life through Adam's sin but was resurrected through Christ's redemption.

Ephesians 2:4–6 emphasizes that it is by God's rich mercy and great love that we, though dead in sins, are made alive with Christ—salvation is entirely by grace through faith, not from ourselves, and certainly not from our works, lest anyone should boast. This deliverance is God's initiative; He seeks out sinners to transform them into His people, illuminated by Christ's light.

No one naturally seeks God while ensnared in sin; it is the Holy Spirit who draws us to respond to the gospel. Anyone believing they have earned salvation through personal deeds is mistaken. Salvation is a divine gift, as affirmed in Acts 16:31 and Ephesians 2:8–10—by grace alone are we saved, through faith, and not by our efforts. This salvation is the work of God, not of humankind.

The Unfathomable Riches of God's Grace

God promises to reveal the depths of His boundless and rich mercy to His people, not just in this life but also in the ages to come. Ephesians 2:7 tells us, "That in the ages to come he might show the exceeding riches of his grace in his kindness toward us through Christ Jesus." It's a profound mystery why God loves us so deeply—sinners who often rebel against His commandments and reject His love.

God's ultimate expression of love is His gift to humanity—Jesus Christ. John 3:16 encapsulates this beautifully: "For God so loved the world, that he gave his only begotten Son, that whosoever believes in him should not perish, but have everlasting life." This scripture illustrates that true love is about giving selflessly, exemplified by God giving His most precious gift, Himself in the person of the Lord Jesus Christ.

Jesus's sacrifice was the ultimate act of selflessness. He gave His life, not just to suffer death but to conquer it, rising on the third day as prophesied, proving His victory over sin and death. This fundamental truth of Christianity is contested by some, including my Muslim brothers and sisters, who deny the crucifixion and resurrection, viewing the Bible as corrupted. While some argue that translation errors have occurred, these do not imply that the Bible itself is corrupt. Rather, many copies of ancient manuscripts remain accessible and reliable for study and reflection.

The intention behind challenging the divinity of Christ and reducing Him to merely a prophet is often to sow doubts among those less familiar with scripture. However, 1 Peter 3:15 urges us to "sanctify the Lord God in your hearts: and be ready always to give an answer to every man that asketh you a reason of the hope that is in you with meekness and fear."

To address claims of contradictions in the Bible, it is crucial to understand that scripture must interpret scripture. Extracting a verse or two as proof texts without considering the full context can lead to misunderstandings. Those not guided by the Spirit may read the texts superficially, but true understanding comes through prayerful study and spiritual guidance.

Satan's attempts to undermine God's Word through deception will ultimately fail. Every student of the Bible should approach it diligently, seeking God's guidance to discern truth from falsehood. I discuss this further in the first chapter of volume one of "Called to be Chosen."

To those of different faiths, I urge you not to be swayed by falsehoods about Jesus Christ. The Bible should be your primary source for understanding His true nature. Contrary to teachings that diminish His role to that of a mere messenger, the Bible affirms His divine nature as detailed in Isaiah 9:6: "And his name shall be called Wonderful, Counselor, The mighty God, The everlasting Father, The Prince of Peace." Any interpretation that denies Christ's deity as a distinct person of the Godhead is misled and misinformed.

Heed the Call: Embrace Salvation Today

If you feel God tugging at your heart, urging you to forsake sin and turn away from other religions towards a pure and undefiled relationship with Him—the God of the Bible and Creator of all—it's crucial to act now. Don't postpone this vital decision for a more convenient moment, waiting until you feel more convinced by the gospel you've encountered. Such a perfect moment may never arrive, and the opportunity for salvation through God could pass by.

Should we pass from this life without the cleansing blood of Christ, without forgiveness for our sins, we face the certainty of divine judgment. The Bible warns of the inevitable destruction that awaits those who persist in rebellion against God. Don't let Satan rob you of the chance to receive the ultimate gift of salvation offered through Jesus Christ.

Be bold and challenge yourself to trust in what the Bible reveals about sin and its remedy. Ask yourself where you stand spiritually before the one true God—a God abounding in mercy, whose very nature is graciousness. He is patient with humanity, yet He has also declared that His Spirit will not contend with man indefinitely. A day will come when the window for salvation closes, and what God seals, no force in the universe and beyond can reopen. I urge you to explore Genesis 6 and Revelation 22 for deeper insight.

CHAPTER 16

CHRIST, YOUR VICTORY

The Spiritual Battle: Resist and Submit

Has anyone tried to resist the devil and found themselves failing repeatedly? Often, this failure occurs because we attempt to fight in our own strength, neglecting to submit fully to God's commandments. Resisting the devil with our own power is not only futile but dangerously misguided. As the Bible warns in James 4:7-8, "Submit yourselves therefore to God. Resist the devil, and he will flee from you. Draw nigh to God, and he will draw nigh to you. Cleanse your hands, ye sinners; and purify your hearts, ye double minded."

Many of us struggle because we only partially submit to God, choosing to live the rest of our lives in disobedience. We seek God's power to escape evil and hardship, yet continue to live by our own rules. This divided living is a direct path to failure; we cannot serve two masters.

Living a life split between God and sin is unsustainable. When we indulge the flesh, the temporary relief soon gives way to pain and regret, leaving deep emotional scars and spiritual wounds. In these moments, we desperately seek God's healing from the consequences of our own choices.

The solution is complete submission to God—not just parts of our lives but all that we are. This full submission allows us to effectively use the Word of God as our defense, saying, "It is written," against Satan's temptations. God invites us to reason with Him, aligning our understanding with His through prayer and scripture, that we might live righteously.

Conversely, Satan tempts us to rationalize sin, to question God's Word, drawing us into a debate on moral relativism. Engaging with these manipulations can quickly lead to sin, as we justify desires that contradict God's laws.

Christians must vigilantly guard their minds, the primary battlefield where spiritual wars are fought. The Bible instructs us in 1 Peter 1:13 to "gird up the loins of your mind, be sober," and in Philippians 4:8 to focus on what is true, honorable, just, pure, lovely, and commendable. These practices shield us from Satan's deceit.

Every person, before being reborn in Christ, lived in sin as a natural state. Those who continue in sin after professing faith must confront the harsh truth that their actions are visible to God, and they cannot hide behind excuses or deceit.

God's urgent call is for repentance, for we may not have another chance. The opportunity to embrace the free gift of salvation through Jesus Christ is now. God examines the hearts of all and will ultimately reward or punish according to our deeds (Jeremiah 17:10 and Revelation 2).

In conclusion, no one can successfully oppose Satan alone. We require the full armor of God, continual prayer, and immersion in Scripture to stand firm. Remember Jesus' assurance in John 16:33, "In the world ye shall have tribulation: but be of good cheer; I have overcome the world."

This ongoing spiritual vigilance and reliance on God's Word and Spirit are essential for overcoming the trials and tribulations of life.

Divine Strength in the Face of Trials

God ensures that His children are not ignorant of the challenges they will face in this life. For those who follow Him, Jesus Christ is the pathway out of the impending destruction that this world faces. As God's co-laborers, believers are tasked with spreading the everlasting gospel of peace to the unsaved, offering them a chance at the saving grace and mercy found in Jesus Christ.

In times of persecution and even when walking through the valley of the shadow of death, God promises to stand by His children. As scripture confirms, "God will comfort us with His rod and with His staff" (Psalms 23:4). The Lord is our refuge and fortress, unshakable by any force in or beyond this universe.

As we grow in Christ, it is crucial to don the whole armor of God continuously, enabling us to withstand the devil's schemes (Ephesians 6:10-17). Be fortified in the Lord and the power of His might, relying on His Word to defend us daily. The importance of constant communion with God cannot be overstated, as outlined in Proverbs 6:20-23, which teaches us to keep His commandments close at heart, guiding us day and night.

Proverbs 3:3-8 also instructs us to embrace mercy and truth, promising that trust in the Lord and rejection of our own understanding will direct our paths and bring health to our being.

The presence of God within us, manifested through the Holy Spirit, assures that we are protected and aided continually. "Greater is He that is in you, than he that is in the world" (1 John 4:4), reminding us of the victory we hold if we remain faithful to Christ. The comfort we derive from knowing that nothing can separate us from the love of God is immense. Romans 8:33-37 celebrates this assurance, proclaiming that in all life's challenges, we are more than conquerors through Him who loved us.

We are encouraged to ground ourselves in the Word of God and set our hearts on heavenly things. Spending time in God's presence should be a joy and an act of worship that pleases Him profoundly. Obedience to Christ's commandments is tantamount to obeying God the Father and the Holy Spirit.

We recognize His voice and follow Him (John 10:27), comforted by the knowledge that our God surpasses all circumstances, powers, and challenges we may encounter. Trusting Him completely means that He will provide for our needs and navigate us through life's trials.

God is ever-present in times of need. His proximity is felt most profoundly when we maintain constant communion and fellowship with Him. Every moment and situation presents an opportunity for worship.

In our journey with God, especially during trials and temptations, the most crucial truth to remember is that our union with Him equips us to overcome any obstacle. His grace is sufficient, His power perfected in our weakness (2 Corinthians 12:9), assuring us that we can endure and prevail, no matter the hardships we face.

CHAPTER 17

WHERE AND HOW DID MANKIND SIN

The Fall of Lucifer: A Tale of Pride and Power

According to the Bible, the origin of sin in the human race traces back to the Garden of Eden as described in Genesis 2 and 3. Created pure by God, Adam and Eve fell into sin due to disobedience, a transgression influenced by Satan, then in the guise of a serpent. This act not only introduced sin to humanity but also marked the beginning of Satan's reign over the sinful world.

Lucifer, as Satan was known before his fall, was created as a perfect being, anointed as a covering cherub who walked among the fiery stones on God's holy mountain (Ezekiel 28:14-16). Gifted with beauty, wisdom, and adorned with precious stones, Lucifer was initially a model of perfection. However, pride led to his downfall. Ezekiel 28:17 tells us that his heart became lifted up because of his beauty, and he corrupted his wisdom due to his brightness, which was a reflection of God's glory, not his own.

Believing himself to be the source of his light, Lucifer aspired to ascend above his station. He envisioned himself equal to God, harboring ambitions to ascend to the heavens and raise his throne above all other angels (Isaiah 14:13-14). His pride and desire for power led him to traffic in sin, defiling his sanctuaries and ultimately leading to his expulsion from God's presence. Ezekiel 28:18 states that God declared He would bring forth a fire from within Lucifer that would consume him and reduce him to ashes upon the Earth.

This narrative highlights a profound mystery of iniquity: how Lucifer, created perfect and dwelling in the presence of God, could harbor sin without external temptation. The Bible indicates that the seeds of rebellion were sown by Lucifer's own gifts, as his beauty and the adulation of his talents filled him with unbridled pride. This internal sin was seen by God, who is omnipresent and all-knowing, and cannot be deceived or usurped.

God's sovereignty is unchallengeable, extending beyond the physical universe to realms unseen. No created being, regardless of their power or beauty, can hope to occupy the throne reserved for God alone, whose presence fills the universe and beyond, and whose qualities are infinite. The ambition of Lucifer to overthrow God was doomed from the start, destined to end in his ultimate defeat and humiliation, as foretold in scriptures.

God's decision to place the tree of knowledge of good and evil in the Garden of Eden was a profound act of giving human beings the freedom of choice. This choice was essential for genuine love and obedience to flourish—qualities that cannot be forced but must be freely given. The presence of this tree was not a setup for failure, but rather a testament to God's respect for human autonomy and His desire for a relationship based on willing devotion rather than compulsion.

Understanding the Fall of Humanity

When Eve, and subsequently Adam, chose to eat from the forbidden tree, they did not just disobey a divine directive—they fundamentally altered the nature of their relationship with God. This act of disobedience was a pivotal moment in human history, leading to what is known in Christian theology as 'The Fall.' By choosing to heed Satan's deception over God's command, they introduced sin into the human experience, severing the intimate connection they enjoyed with their Creator. This separation from God brought about spiritual and eventually physical death, as the direct presence and sustaining power of God were withdrawn.

The Consequences of Disobedience

The immediate effect of Adam and Eve's sin was spiritual death, as stated in Genesis 3. They lost the light of divine life that had illuminated their existence, plunging into a state of spiritual darkness. This loss is reflected in their sudden awareness of their nakedness and their attempt to cover themselves with fig leaves—a symbolic representation of their newfound vulnerability and shame. The spiritual death was a precursor to physical mortality, marking the beginning of decay and death in the physical world.

Satan's Temporary Rule

By disobeying God and obeying Satan, humanity unwittingly granted Satan temporary authority over the world. This shift is critical in understanding the state of the world as described in subsequent biblical texts, where Satan is referred to as "the prince of this world" (John 12:31). His rule is characterized by deception, strife, and alienation from God. However, it's important to note that this authority is limited and ultimately subject to God's sovereign will.

The Role of Free Will

The narrative of Adam and Eve underscores a fundamental aspect of human existence—the power and responsibility of free will. God's creation of humans with the ability to choose is a theme echoed throughout the Bible, demonstrating His desire for a relationship with humanity grounded in genuine love and voluntary submission.

Divine Justice and Mercy

Throughout Scripture, God is depicted as perfectly just and infinitely merciful. The tests and commandments He sets before humanity are not arbitrary but are designed to lead us towards living in harmony with His righteous standards. Psalms and Deuteronomy affirm God's perfect nature and His just actions, reinforcing the belief that His laws are set not to ensnare us but to liberate us from the bondage of sin.

In summary, the introduction of the tree of knowledge of good and evil was a divine setup for testing human obedience and fostering a depth of relationship that only true freedom can facilitate. It highlighted the importance of obedience to God's commandments, the devastating consequences of sin, and the overarching theme of God's justice interwoven with His mercy. This narrative sets the stage for the need for redemption—a theme that culminates in the New Testament with the sacrificial death and resurrection of Jesus Christ, who overcomes the power of sin and death, thus restoring the broken relationship between God and humanity.

Satan's Role as the Accuser

God's intent was never to deceive mankind, in stark contrast to Satan, who embodies evil and wickedness. As the Bible reveals, Satan perpetually seeks to undermine God's righteousness, even accusing Him before the celestial courts

(Revelation 12:10). He famously challenged God's motives in the tale of Job, questioning, "Doth Job serve God for nought?" (Job 1:9). This accusation implies a deeper slander against God's design of human free will, suggesting that humanity might lack the genuine choice to serve God or Satan.

The Gift of Free Will

Despite Satan's claims, the Biblical narrative affirms that God endowed mankind with the clear capacity to choose between good and evil. This is exemplified in the Edenic commandment given to Adam and Eve, setting the foundational precedent for moral decision-making (Genesis 2:16-17). Thus, the ability to choose is a divine gift, not a predetermined condition as Satan might allege.

The Power Dynamics Between God and Satan

Satan's attempts to thwart God's purposes are ultimately futile. Created as a finite being with limits to his power, Satan cannot alter the fundamental nature of creation. Although Scripture acknowledges that Satan was granted considerable might, it remains minuscule compared to the infinite power of God. This inherent limitation underscores a crucial theological point: Satan operates within the parameters God allows (Job 1:12).

Conclusion

Understanding the stark contrasts between God's infinite power and Satan's limited scope helps clarify the ongoing spiritual battle depicted in the Bible. It reinforces the Christian doctrine that while Satan may be a formidable adversary, his capabilities are ultimately restricted by God's sovereign will. The awareness of Satan's role and the reality of free will can empower believers to make informed choices in their spiritual lives, aligning with God's righteousness rather than succumbing to deception.

Free Will and the Human Condition

God created humans and angels with the capacity for choice, not as automatons without free will. This foundational aspect of God's creation emphasizes His sufficiency and completeness. He does not need creation to fill a void; instead, He created the universe for His pleasure and glory. Each person possesses an innate understanding of God's existence and the moral dichotomy of right and wrong. This knowledge equips us to choose obedience to God or disobedience, aligning with Satan (Genesis 2:16-17).

The Fall and Its Consequences

Human history is marred by the choice to disobey God, a decision that introduced sin and its ramifications into the world—as described in Romans 5:12, "Wherefore, as by one man sin entered the world, and death by sin; and so death passed upon all men, for that all have sinned." Despite this fall, God did not abandon humanity to its fate but provided a redemptive solution through Jesus Christ before the world's foundation was laid. This salvation is vividly described in Romans 5:15, offering grace and redemption to all who accept Christ.

The Redemption and New Birth

The transformative power of Christ's sacrifice allows those who believe to become "sons of God," born not of human will but of God (John 1:12-13). This new birth grants us a spirit that seeks to fulfill God's will, contrasting sharply with our carnal nature, which inclines towards sin.

Dual Nature and Spiritual Warfare

As believers, we exist with dual natures: the carnal, governed by the flesh, and the spiritual, influenced by our new nature in Christ. These are in constant conflict, as described in Romans 7. The law of the flesh wars against the law of the spirit, compelling us towards sin. However, through Christ, we have the strength to overcome these earthly desires and live according to God's spiritual law.

Conclusion

In conclusion, though we struggle with sin due to our carnal nature, the redemption offered through Christ enables us to overcome and align with God's will. By crucifying our fleshly desires and focusing on the spiritual, we can live lives of righteousness, ultimately fulfilling God's purpose for us. Let us, therefore, embrace the spiritual life, acknowledging the daily battle between flesh and spirit but relying on God's grace to triumph.

CHAPTER 18

YOUR SUCCESS IS IN CHRIST

Overcoming Discouragement and Procrastination through Faith

Discouragement and procrastination are not merely obstacles to personal success; they are spiritual battles that many Christians face. These forces can prevent believers from realizing the life God intends for them. It is essential to recognize that God has equipped us with all we need to overcome these challenges and excel (Ephesians 2:10). However, misuse of God's gifts can lead to negative consequences, even affecting future generations. Therefore, it's crucial to live in obedience and make choices that align with God's will.

The Power of Positive Influences

Surrounding ourselves with godly, positive influences is vital for spiritual growth and success. Listening to and engaging with those who embody Christ's teachings helps us to avoid the pitfalls of negativity and backward movement. Remember, "As iron sharpens iron, so one person sharpens another" (Proverbs 27:17). If you find yourself the smartest in your group, it might be time to seek new associations that can challenge and inspire you to grow in faith and action.

Living a Life of Discipleship

Philippians 3:14 reminds us to "press toward the mark for the prize of the high calling of God in Christ Jesus." This scripture is not just about personal advancement but calls us to live out the abundant life Christ offers here on Earth. It is our duty to use our gifts not for self-promotion but to bless others and advance the kingdom of God. This involves active discipleship, teaching, and mentoring others as Christ did, with selflessness and compassion.

Conclusion: A Call to Selfless Service

In conclusion, let us embrace the challenges of discipleship, recognizing that although there is a cost, it pales in comparison to the consequences of inaction. Let's commit to using our blessings to bless others, fulfilling our role as Christ's disciples in a world that desperately needs godly influence and the message of peace found in the gospel.

Defining Good Success

Good success in the Christian life is fundamentally built upon the Word of God. It involves living out virtues like honesty, integrity, and fairness—traits that are developed through adherence to biblical teachings. Such success ensures that God receives all credit for our achievements, recognizing His omniscience and omnipotence in our lives.

The Stewardship of Divine Gifts

God has endowed each of us with unique talents and abilities, intending that we use them to honor Him. This stewardship is not merely a responsibility but a privilege. We must guard against using these gifts for selfish ends, which leads to spiritual corruption and can have widespread negative effects, including generational curses. The misuse of divine gifts mirrors the biblical account of Lucifer, whose initial endowments were meant for God's glory but became tools of rebellion.

Lucifer's Fall and Its Lessons

Lucifer, created as an anointed cherub, was adorned with unmatched beauty and gifted with powerful abilities, standing in the presence of God (Ezekiel 28:14-17). Yet, he succumbed to pride, desiring worship that belonged only to God. This narrative serves as a stern warning: no matter how gifted, we must remain humble and use our abilities to serve God faithfully.

The Bible does not provide complete details of God's interactions with Lucifer before his rebellion. However, based on God's revealed nature as merciful and forgiving, it is plausible to think that God would have offered Lucifer forgiveness had he repented. This reflection on divine mercy underscores the importance of humility and repentance in our spiritual journeys.

Application to Our Lives

Each Christian is called to reflect on these biblical lessons. By evaluating our attitudes towards our own gifts and talents, we can ensure they are used in ways that glorify God rather than feed our pride. In doing so, we not only avoid the pitfalls that befell Lucifer but also advance God's kingdom on Earth through genuine acts of service and discipleship.

Lucifer: The Light Bearer and His Fall

The Gift of Wisdom and the Corruption Thereof

Lucifer was endowed with exceptional wisdom, surpassing all other created beings, a gift from his Creator, reflecting the light of Christ Himself. His very name, meaning "light bearer," signifies his original purpose—to reflect the divine light and truth of Jesus Christ (Ezekiel 28:15). However, his perception of himself as the source rather than a mere conduit of this light marked the inception of his iniquity.

Lucifer's Role and Rebellion

Tasked with a sacred role, Lucifer's vocal abilities were divinely tuned to produce heavenly music, glorifying God among the celestial assembly. Yet, pride stemming from his unique gifts led him to aspire beyond his role as a servant. He envisioned himself equal to the Most High, aiming to usurp God's unapproachable position (Isaiah 14:13-14).

The Omnipotence and Sovereignty of God

In stark contrast to Lucifer's rebellion, the scripture reaffirms the unrivaled power of God. He alone stretched out the heavens and laid the foundations of the earth without any assistance (Isaiah 40:22, Isaiah 55:11). God's words are not idle—they manifest reality, achieving exactly what He intends, underscoring His ultimate authority over all creation.

The Finite Versus the Infinite

While Lucifer was a pinnacle of creation, his essence and capabilities remain finite. In contrast, God exists outside the dimensions of time and space He created. He is infinite, omnipresent, and omniscient—attributes that no created being can ever attain. Lucifer's desire to overthrow God highlights the futility and folly of contesting the divine will (Job 38:4-7).

Conclusion: Theological Implications and Modern Reflections

Understanding the narrative of Lucifer's fall serves as a sobering reminder of the dangers of pride and self-glorification. For believers, it reinforces the necessity of humility and reliance on God's sovereignty. As we reflect on our own spiritual journeys, let us recognize our limitations and the grace that sustains us, ensuring we use our God-given gifts to glorify Him, not ourselves

Introduction: Understanding Rebellion and Divine Judgment

The narrative of Lucifer's fall and the subsequent temptation of Christ encapsulates profound lessons about rebellion, divine judgment, and the nature of true success. This exploration delves into the theological implications of these events and their relevance to believers today.

The Temptation of Christ and Lucifer's Rebellion

In the wilderness, Satan attempted to usurp the worship due only to God by tempting Christ with earthly power (Matthew 4:1-11). This act mirrored his earlier deception with Adam and Eve, which resulted in humanity's fall and the usurpation of earthly dominion. Scripture illustrates that these actions stem from a pattern of lies and rebellion initiated by Lucifer, once a bearer of light and now a purveyor of darkness.

Divine Retribution and Final Judgment

Scripture foretells a stern judgment for Lucifer and his followers, emphasizing the irreversible consequences of their rebellion. Ezekiel 28 and Revelation detail the ultimate destruction of Satan—cast out and reduced to ashes as a spectacle to all creation. This narrative serves as a warning: the divine patience is vast but not indefinite, and the window for repentance has a closure.

Practical Implications for Believers

For believers, these narratives underscore the necessity of humility, stewardship, and alignment with God's will. The gifts we receive are not for personal glorification but for the service of God's kingdom. Misuse of these gifts not only leads to personal downfall but also affects the wider community.

Conclusion: The Path to True Success

True success is defined not by worldly standards but by fidelity to divine principles. It requires diligence, humility, and a commitment to godly principles—traits starkly absent in Lucifer's conduct. As we pursue success, let it be grounded in truth, righteousness, and the joy that comes from serving God faithfully.

Some people seek success with minimal effort, quick to blame others for their failures. They lack the honesty to acknowledge their own shortcomings, evident in their reluctance to face the truth about themselves. They desire the rewards of success without enduring its challenges, wanting to reach the finish line without participating in the race. They aspire to lead their lives in the wrong direction, yet still expect others to guide them towards true success.

My friend, remember, there are no free lunches in life. True success requires diligent work and a clear plan of action, aligning with God's commands. We are endowed by God with all necessary attributes for success at creation, but sin has buried these gifts deep within us. It is only through God's grace that these can be unearthed, allowing the true beauty of His gifts to illuminate our lives and glorify Him. Those yet to embrace God's transformation must seek His guidance to reflect Christ's image.

As God's people, we must wisely utilize everything He has entrusted to us to achieve godly success. This entails diligent stewardship and commitment to our heavenly Father's work, striving for success in all life areas. We need to discard outdated beliefs and embrace new teachings led by the Holy Spirit through the Word of God. Our minds must be renewed to think beyond a sluggard's mindset.

Strategically investing the gifts and talents God has bestowed upon us is essential for yielding a return on His investments, enriching our lives and the kingdom of God. If unsure of our talents, we should ask God, who will reveal them. These talents often manifest in our natural abilities, such as teaching, writing God-inspired music, or embodying Christ's likeness as a beacon of godliness.

Our power stems from God, and without connection to Him, we are powerless. As Jesus said, "Without me, you can do nothing" (John 15:5). We must avoid the pitfall of unbelief, where talents and gifts are buried instead of being nurtured in faith. Laziness and sloth can impede our spiritual growth and block the blessings meant for us.

Every Christian should aim to be productive, resisting discouragement and temptation. By seeking God through prayer and His Word, our efforts will be amplified by heavenly support. Diligence is crucial; we cannot afford to be idle, allowing others to reap the rewards of their hard work while we covet their success. True success demands time and effort, in accordance with Biblical teachings.

Our gifts should positively impact our surroundings, spreading the gospel through our actions. Hard work, combined with diligence and adherence to God's Word, leads to abundant rewards. Successful individuals joyfully sow the seeds God has given them, diligently nurturing their growth according to His plan. Conversely, those who choose merely to exist, acting parasitically or covetously, engage in behaviors that are not only destructive but sinful.

Actions of greed and envy, deeply ingrained in many churches today, are manifestations of demonic influences, as they oppose the commandment in Exodus 20:17 not to covet. Those who covet often overlook the sacrifices behind another's achievements—sacrifices marked by heartache, sweat, tears, and countless errors.

However, it is our duty, as recipients of God's blessings through hard work, to mentor those who have not yet realized their potential. We are called to help them discover and achieve success through the gifts and talents God has bestowed upon them. Indeed, the fruits of one's own labor are far more satisfying than coveting another's.

God has endowed every individual with unique gifts and talents, aligning with their specific skills and abilities. He created no one without purpose; each person is meant to glorify Him. Yet, often, people limit themselves, choosing mundane or even destructive paths. They misuse their God-given talents to do evil instead of good.

Christian scientists, for instance, exemplify the use of God-given intellect to explore and understand the world, recognizing the divine design behind the universe. Their studies reaffirm the rational belief in an intelligent Creator, countering the notion that life could arise from non-life through mere chance.

We, the faithful, are convinced by the Holy Spirit of the incredible complexity with which God has designed every human being. We are just beginning to understand the complexities of life, especially the human body, which stands as the pinnacle of complexity among all living things on Earth.

God's true nature is so holy that it consumes anything tainted with sin. His unapproachable brightness fills the universe, and yet, He remains beyond the confines of the heavens. The cherubim covering the Ark of the Covenant shield their eyes from His glory, which illuminates every corner of the cosmos.

The vastness and complexity of God's existence are beyond human comprehension; no language can fully capture His essence. However, through Jesus Christ—God revealed—mankind can glimpse the nature of our Creator, in whose image we are made. Jesus not only reveals God's glory but also provides a way for us to withstand the brilliance of His purity.

Christ is God with us, as declared in Matthew 1:23. By becoming man, yet without relinquishing His divinity, Jesus embraced humanity's sinful condition—a condition that began when mankind first disobeyed their Creator. Despite His human limitations, Jesus maintained His omniscient and omnipresent nature, exemplifying the ultimate servant leader without sin. The responsibility of governance was His, as foretold in Isaiah 9:6.

No one is better equipped than you to fulfill the specific role God has called you to. You are uniquely valuable in God's eyes. Stay focused on Christ, adhere to His teachings, and you will achieve success in every aspect of your life. The talents and abilities God grants us are meant to advance His kingdom and glorify our Creator.

If any Christian is not using their gifts for these purposes, they should seek God's forgiveness today. Now is the time to steward the gifts you've received from God to glorify Him. God desires all His children to thrive and succeed, but only through His righteous and holy ways.

In Christ, we have everything, for He embodies the fullness of life and possesses everything we need. The Holy Spirit guides and teaches us how to achieve godly success and to act rightly before God and others.

God educates His people about the truth of His creation and counsels us on living righteously. Those who stray from God's path are vulnerable to Satan's attacks. Stubbornness and ignorance are not what destroy us; rather, it is the deadly arrows of unbelief, fear, and doubt—tools of Satan.

Without God's complete armor, we are exposed to these attacks. The smallest opening is enough for Satan to devastate lives. Remember, the Holy Spirit is the ultimate helper in times of need.

We must never forget the source of our blessings and success. Always give thanks to God for His indescribable mercy and grace. If you've faltered in the past, God provides opportunities to start anew, guided by the knowledge you've gained. As Proverbs 14:12 warns, seeking our way apart from God leads to destruction.

Patience is a virtue God teaches us, especially when we don't immediately see His blessings. Trust in Him, even when others seem more favored. Do not let envy cloud your perspective. God has the perfect solution for your challenges, even if the timing and method are unclear. Remember, setbacks are just one chapter in your life story; a better ending awaits. Your success often depends on your attitude towards the challenges you face.

If it offers any comfort, I want you, the reader, to know that I stand with you in prayer. I ask God to strengthen the faith He has given you, trusting Him as the sovereign Lord of your life. When we endure life's struggles—which God uses to prepare us for greater blessings—we must remember that all things work together for our good if we love the Lord and persevere in our faith (Romans 8:28).

The Scripture encourages us to rejoice always, regardless of our circumstances (Philippians 4:4). This command is not about ignoring our struggles but recognizing that God is refining us for a higher purpose. Those who patiently wait on the Lord will find their strength renewed, soaring on wings like eagles, running without growing weary (Isaiah 40:31). This process isn't merely about waiting; it's about deeply trusting God's timing and wisdom.

Amidst the storms of life, keep your eyes on God, not the chaos around you. Focusing on the storm will only bring fear and doubt, potentially overwhelming you with discouragement.

As followers of Christ, we are also admonished to avoid unnecessary debt (Romans 13:8). Our society often equates possessions with personal value, pushing many into spending beyond their means to impress others. This is not just unwise—it is living a lie. I have learned through personal experience that with little, God can accomplish much. By rejecting the urge to keep up appearances and choosing instead to live within our means, we allow God to teach us contentment and stewardship.

Moreover, tithing is not merely a duty but a profound expression of faith. It challenges our conventional understanding of security and provision. Even when faced with dire needs, placing God first may require sacrificial giving, which defies human logic. However, this act of faith invites God's supernatural intervention. Trusting God with the little we have, and obeying Him in our giving, allows God to multiply our humble offerings beyond measure.

We are called to give God the first tenth of all our increase, honoring Him with the first fruits of our labor—not the leftovers. Tithing is an act of worship, done in a spirit of gratitude and joy. When we hold back, we not only rob God but also deprive ourselves, stifling our own potential for success. Giving our first and best to God ensures that our offerings are pure and pleasing to Him, free from stinginess or reluctance.

God generously provides us with everything we need to fulfill the roles He has assigned to us. There is no shortfall too great for Him to bridge; He fills the gap between our current resources and our potential. We are equipped with unique gifts and talents specifically designed to glorify God and serve as a testament to His grace and mercy to those who do not yet know Him. Through Christ's redemption, we are empowered to be proactive, successful contributors in God's kingdom.

Do not fret over the mechanisms of your success. Trust that God has designed the perfect path for you, and He will provide all that you need to prosper. He uses life's challenges to strengthen our faith and opens doors for us to apply our skills in ways that honor Him. God knows our needs intimately, and He promises to supply just the right measure for us to achieve greatness in His name.

As followers of Christ, God is our sole provider. He has placed resources on Earth for us to use wisely and productively. By preparing ourselves with the necessary skills and adopting a mindset of readiness, we position ourselves to receive God's planned blessings. Patience and prayer are key as we await God's timing, which is always perfect. His strategies for our lives are uniquely tailored to fit our individual journeys.

To truly witness God's hand at work in our lives, we must trust Him completely, surrendering every aspect of our being to His will. This complete trust is not passive but involves active engagement with our faith, continually seeking to align our actions with God's desires for us.

Godly Successful Marriages

God intends marriage to embody unconditional love, sacrifice, honor, respect, and responsibility—mirroring the relationship between Christ and His church. In this divine union, two distinct individuals are joined as one in holy matrimony, reflecting the profound mystery and sanctity of their bond.

However, Christians have different opinions about marriage, especially when it comes to same-sex unions. Based on traditional readings of scripture, such as 1 Corinthians 6:9–10 and Romans 1, these relationships are understood by, we, orthodox Bible believing Christians as incompatible with God's plan. These texts and others in the Old Testament are often used to show that variations from this model do not match God's purposes for marriage.

The orthodox Christian belief is not a contentious one nor an interpretation issue, but our belief is based on the clear clarification of the Bible being its own interpreter. God says in Genesis 2:24: "Therefore shall a man leave his father and his mother, and shall cleave unto his wife: and they shall be one flesh." Reading this scripture in its full context where God is our parent, there is no ambiguity of what God is saying. He made our first parents male and female. It takes a mother (woman) and a father (man) to form what God defines marriage is.

God does not change and neither does His Word. They are one in the same. God defines marriage in the beginning as we see in the scripture cited in the previous paragraph in clear distinct language that He uses to make sure mankind gets what He is saying. This clarity is brought out in the full context in the verses surrounding Genesis 2:24.

It is essential to approach these discussions with the utmost care and respect for all individuals. While maintaining fidelity to what many believe the scriptures teach, it is also crucial to engage with those who hold different views with compassion and understanding, recognizing the dignity of every person. And so God is very clear about the definition of marriage that He is telling the church to obey. God is not the Author of confusion. Satan is. And he has the church all twisted up and confused with very flawed interpretations of a simple commandment God wants His children and the rest of mankind to obey.

The Nature of Sin and Choice

Scripture teaches that God despises sin but loves the sinner, offering redemption and transformation through Christ. This belief underscores the Christian call to separate sin from the individual, encouraging repentance and a return to godliness. In matters of personal choice, scripture asserts that individuals are endowed with free will, responsible for their decisions and their consequences (Matthew 19:4–6, Ephesians 6, Genesis 2:23–24).

Engagement with Societal Views

In today's world, terms like "hate" and "homophobia" are sometimes used to critique traditional Christian beliefs. It is important for Christians to articulate their positions based on scripture without appearing to compromise on compassion and empathy. This involves presenting biblical truths in a manner that is both firm and loving, ensuring that discussions are grounded in a deep understanding of God's word, which is seen as unchanging and absolute.

Responding to Alternative Interpretations

Some within the church have reinterpreted biblical texts to accommodate modern societal changes. While it is vital to address these interpretations, it should be done with a spirit of humility and a willingness to engage in meaningful dialogue. Asserting the consistency of God's word across both Testaments, Christians believe that God's standards of righteousness and sin do not change.

The Role of the Christian Community

As members of the Christian community, it is our duty to uphold the teachings of the Bible as we understand them, while also reaching out with a message of love and redemption. The church's mission is to reflect God's truth and grace in all interactions, serving as a beacon of hope and moral clarity in a confused and searching world.

Godly Successful Marriages

God's design for marriage is beautifully exemplified in Genesis 2, where He united Adam and Eve, setting the foundation for marital unions between a godly man with traditional Christian values and a godly woman with traditional Christian values. As a testament to this divine institution, my wife and I strive daily to embody the unity and love that God intends for all marriages as defined in the Word of God. We recognize that perfection may be unattainable in this life, but that does not mean that we should not strive for it for it is God who said in Matthew 5:48: "Be ye therefore perfect, even as your Father which is in heaven is perfect". What God is saying is that the children of God must always be in a state of becoming perfect. Being in this mind-set sets the minds of the true children of God on heavenly things. Thus, heavenly things have eternal value as opposed to earthly things which shall be destroyed by God in the judgment of Jesus' Christ. It is through mutual understanding, continuous effort, and God's grace, we navigate the complexities of married life.

We have learned to forget the failures of yesterday and look for God's promises in tomorrow and beyond. We honor our marriages and cling to the blessings God has given us—each other and the gifts in our relationship. Marriage needs self-investment; it needs love, understanding, and forgiveness, like caring for children or other dependents. It needs the husband and the wife to give their all. Two partners are much stronger than one alone, as they can face challenges better and make a strong home.

As believers, we are called not just to maintain our marriages but to actively strengthen them against any forces that might threaten their stability. This involves tearing down strongholds that suffocate and strangle our relationships and building up defenses through spiritual unity and prayer. My wife and I continually seek the Holy Spirit's guidance to fortify our bond, ensuring that it withstands the inevitable storms of life.

With God at the center, married couples are sealed internally by the Holy Spirit and externally by the protective grace of Christ. This divine coverage prevents the world's corruptions from infiltrating the sacred space of marriage and keeps the blessings God has instilled from leaking out, even amid life's most tumultuous storms. For one man, rain might bring floods of destruction; for another, the same rains can be showers of blessings.

The principles of godly marriage extend beyond visible love to the deeper, sometimes challenging, dynamics of submission and sacrificial love. As husbands, we are called to love our wives as Christ loved the church—selflessly and unconditionally—even when faced with difficulties. This kind of love can transform relationships and bear witness to the transformative power of God's love.

Yet, many find it challenging to submit their wills to God's commands. Successful marriages require total yielding to God's design, both in how spouses treat each other and in their personal walk with God. If we struggle to submit to a God we cannot see, how much more challenging can it be to consistently demonstrate love and humility toward our spouse?

God does not change; His standards for sin and righteousness remain consistent throughout the scriptures. As Christians, we are called to uphold these truths, while also reaching out with compassion and understanding to those who view these matters differently. Engaging in discussions about difficult topics requires grace and truth, a balance that reflects our commitment to God's word and His love for all people.

Godly Successful Marriages

Marriage, as divinely established in the Garden of Eden and affirmed by Christ's relationship with the church, is intended to be a lifelong union between a man and a woman. This sacred covenant is not just about loving companionship but also about fostering spiritual fellowship with each other under God's guidance each day.

In our commitment to uphold the biblical view of marriage, it is crucial to remember that marriage involves more than physical or material attributes. While societal trends might emphasize external qualities or financial status, Christian marriage calls us to look deeper. God values the condition of the heart above all else. Therefore, when considering a partner, it's essential to see beyond the surface and evaluate the spiritual and character alignment with biblical principles.

For believers, the Scripture is clear: Do not be unequally yoked with unbelievers (2 Corinthians 6:14). This guidance is not about exclusion but about ensuring mutual spiritual support and growth within the marriage. Choosing a spouse who shares a common faith and belief in the triune God—Father, Son, and Holy Spirit—is foundational for a marriage that seeks to glorify God.

Moreover, marriage is not a transaction or a mere partnership; it is a total commitment, mirroring Christ's complete dedication to His church. Christ did not give half of Himself for our redemption; He gave all. His sacrificial love sets the ultimate standard for marital love and commitment. The union of marriage is not about giving 50 percent but about each partner giving their whole self to the other, just as Christ did for the church.

Sadly, many marriages today are built on less substantial grounds, which may explain why some do not endure. When marriages are formed based on superficial criteria, they are less likely to withstand the challenges that life brings. It's troubling that such trends are also prevalent within the church. This underscores the need for sound biblical teaching and strong pastoral guidance to help believers make wise, godly decisions about marriage.

As we live out our marriages, let us strive to be true reflections of Christ's love and fidelity. This means continually working on our own character and spiritual growth, being genuine and authentic in our actions, and allowing God's Word to transform us from the inside out. Our marriages should not be showcases of perfection but testimonies of God's grace and ongoing work in our lives.

Let us discard any facade of "phony Christianity" and embrace a life that truly bears the fragrance of Christ, demonstrating His love, grace, and truth in every aspect of our lives, especially in our marriages. This is how we witness to the world—not just through our words but through the authenticity of our relationships and the genuine love we display, both publicly and privately.

The Marriage Supper of the Lamb: A Model for Our Marriages

Revelation 19:7 foretells the marriage supper of the Lamb, symbolizing the union between Christ and His church. Christ's submission to God's will—even to the point of death—underscores His profound love and commitment. This act was not just a sacrifice but a declaration of His willingness to become one with humanity, fully embracing both His deity and humanity without reservation.

In this divine example, we find the ultimate model for marriage. Just as Christ gave 100 percent of Himself, so too must husbands and wives commit fully to their union. Marriage is not about maintaining individual agendas but about coming together, humbling oneself, submitting to God's will, and sacrificing personal pride for the sake of the relationship.

Living Out the Fruits of the Spirit in Marriage

The fruit of the Spirit—love, joy, peace, forbearance, kindness, goodness, faithfulness, gentleness, and self-control—are essential in reflecting God's presence in our marriages. When couples live according to these virtues, they fortify their marriage against the incursions of selfishness, manipulation, and disrespect.

Conversely, living according to the flesh, detached from the spiritual guidance of God's Word, can lead to discord and dissatisfaction within the marriage. As a tree is known by its fruit, so too is the quality of our marriages revealed through our actions and choices.

Commitment to Growth and Unity

Marriage requires dedication and hard work from both partners. It involves more than just emotional investment; it requires a daily commitment to grow and nurture the relationship in accordance with God's principles. Veterans of marriage will attest to the challenges and the hard work involved, but also to the profound joys and blessings that a God-led marriage can bring.

This sacred institution is not only a personal commitment but a covenant before God, mirroring the holy union between Christ and His church as described in Ephesians 5:22–33 and Hebrews 13:4. As such, marriage is a profound commitment to walk together not just in companionship but in spiritual fellowship, striving each day to embody the love Christ has shown us.

Invitation to Reflect and Act

Let us then approach marriage not as a contract to be entered into lightly but as a covenant that reflects Christ's covenant with us. May our marriages be a testament to the sacrificial, redeeming love of Christ, filled with the grace and truth that He embodies. And let us support one another in this journey, offering encouragement, wisdom, and compassion as we walk together in the light of His Word.

Your situation, God has provided the pathway for success that aligns with His divine plans and purposes for you. As we strive to fulfill God's call in every aspect of our lives, be it as single individuals, married couples, or parents, our ultimate aim should be to reflect His love and righteousness.

Revised Manuscript Sections:

Godly Successful Single People

Living successfully as a single person in Christ involves honoring God with your body and spirit. This includes seeking God's timing and wisdom in finding a spouse if you feel called to marriage. The Bible teaches us to wait on the Lord and trust His plans (Psalm 27:14). During this period of singleness, focus on deepening your relationship with God and understanding His Word, which provides the guidance needed for every decision.

It's crucial to remember that the desires God places in our hearts may often contrast sharply with our fleshly desires. To truly walk in the Spirit, our wills and carnal desires must be surrendered to God daily. This means living a life of self-denial and sacrifice, allowing God to shape our desires to align with His perfect will. As 1 Peter 5:10 promises, after enduring trials for a while, God Himself will perfect, establish, strengthen, and settle you.

Godly Successful Children

Raising children in a godly manner is one of the most significant challenges and blessings. According to Scriptures like Deuteronomy 6:4–9 and Proverbs 22:6, we are tasked with the responsibility of teaching our children the ways of the Lord. This involves more than just instruction; it requires embodying the principles of the Bible in our everyday actions.

Children are keen observers and will model their behavior on what they see at home. Therefore, our lives must be consistent with the teachings of Scripture. This is not solely the responsibility of schools or society but primarily falls on parents and guardians. Remember, even if past mistakes have been made in parenting, God provides opportunities for redemption and new beginnings.

Every challenge in parenting is an opportunity for growth—both for the parent and the child. By relying on the Holy Spirit's guidance, parents can impart wisdom, discipline, and love, preparing children to face the world with a firm foundation in Christ.

Conclusion

For singles, married couples, and parents alike, success in God's eyes is about more than worldly achievements; it involves growing in faith, fostering godly relationships, and living out His commandments. By placing Him at the center of our lives and seeking His wisdom daily through prayer and Scripture, we align ourselves with His purposes.

Whether you are guiding a child, nurturing a marriage, or pursuing personal holiness in singleness, remember that all things are possible through Christ who strengthens us (Philippians 4:13). Let us then approach each role and challenge with faith, patience, and an unwavering trust in God's perfect plan for our lives.

Abraham: An Earthly Example of Success

God's call to Abram, transforming him into Abraham—the "father of many nations"—serves as a profound example of what it means to live a life of faith and obedience. Abraham's journey from his homeland to an unfamiliar territory signifies a leap of faith that all believers are called to emulate. This leap is not just physical but spiritual, requiring us to leave behind our old ways and trust wholly in God's promises.

Abraham's life teaches us that true success is rooted in complete dependence on God. It's about surrendering our plans to His will and believing in His good and perfect provisions. As Abraham did, when we let go of our past and reach forward to what lies ahead, we press toward the mark for the prize of the high calling of God in Christ Jesus.

This biblical narrative is not just historical but highly relevant today. In a world rife with dishonesty—from academic cheating to corporate fraud—the call to live with integrity is both urgent and necessary. Like Abraham, we are to navigate our lives with honesty and a pure heart, which not only pleases God but also sets a standard in a world searching for moral clarity.

Practical Implications for Today

For us today, living like Abraham means making decisions that reflect integrity and patience, rather than succumbing to the quick and easy paths that may lead to unethical outcomes. Whether in business, education, or personal relationships, the principle of doing everything with a spirit of excellence and faithfulness to God's word holds the key to true success.

Moreover, as we engage with the world, let us be beacons of God's truth, showing through our actions that success doesn't compromise with dishonesty. Our commitment to living out God's commands should be evident in how we treat others, manage responsibilities, and uphold justice.

Promises for the Faithful

Christ's promises, as reflected in the Beatitudes, assure us of God's blessings not only in the hereafter but in our present lives. Being "meek" and "pure in heart" are not signs of weakness but of strength, offering us a guide to inheriting the earth and seeing God in our daily lives.

As believers, if we walk in faith and acknowledge Christ in all areas of our lives, we are assured of a victorious existence on earth—a life marked not by temporary triumphs but by lasting spiritual fulfillment and divine peace.

By integrating these teachings into our lives, we not only follow in the footsteps of Abraham but also fulfill the covenant of grace and mercy established through Jesus Christ. This covenant promises not just eternal life but a profoundly abundant life here on earth, guiding us through every challenge and blessing us in ways beyond our comprehension.

The Call to Transformation

God's call to change from who we are to who He desires us to be—children of the Most High—is a profound journey of faith, similar to Abraham's. This walk with God is not just about avoiding sin; it's about embracing a life filled with His blessings and becoming a beacon of His grace to the world.

God invites everyone to turn from sin and embrace the salvation offered through Jesus Christ. This isn't merely about following rules; it's about becoming vessels of His righteousness, displaying the fruit of His Spirit in every aspect of our lives. By accepting Christ, you become a living testament to the Gospel, influencing others not through coercion, but through the compelling witness of a transformed life.

Submitting to God's Will

James 4:6-7 and 1 Peter 5:6-7 teach us that victory over sin and Satan comes only through submission to God. This submission must be complete and humble, acknowledging our inability to succeed alone. Every time we try to handle life in our own strength, we fall short. However, when we fully surrender to God, allowing His Spirit to guide and strengthen us, we find that obstacles become opportunities for growth and victory.

Submitting to God means casting all our cares upon Him, trusting that He cares for us deeply and personally. It means letting go of pride and self-reliance and embracing a life of dependence on God's grace and power.

Living a Successful Christian Life

True success in the Christian life involves more than outward achievements—it's about being successful in God's eyes. This success is marked by a life lived in accordance with God's Word, a life that exudes faith, integrity, and love regardless of circumstances.

Being "in Christ" means that our old ways of thinking and behaving are replaced by new patterns that reflect God's character. We must be courageous, not conforming to the world's standards but transforming them by renewing our minds (Romans 12:2). This transformation is evident in how we view and respond to life's challenges—we see them as God sees them, opportunities for growth and testimonies of His power.

The Impact of a Faithful Life

A life lived in faith is not without its challenges. Success can bring opposition and jealousy from unexpected quarters. Yet, we are called not to focus on these trials but to remain steadfast in our commitment to God's purpose. Remember, "Blessed are the meek, for they shall inherit the earth" (Matthew 5:5). The purity of our hearts will allow us to see God more clearly and to experience His presence more fully.

So, let us press on, not with mere words of praise but with hearts fully committed to God. Let us live our lives in such a way that they testify to the reality of His transforming power, showing that with God, all things are possible, and indeed, more abundant.

Triumph Over Trials

As followers of Christ, we are called to a life of victory, not exempt from challenges, but equipped to overcome them through faith. Understand that Satan's opposition is a confirmation that we are aligned with God's purpose—our advancements in life are often met with resistance from those who prefer our stagnation. However, remember that God uses our journey to inspire and motivate others. Never retreat nor diminish the spiritual elevation God grants because it serves as a beacon of hope and a testament to His power.

God's Unfailing Support

No challenge is too great for God. Whether it's illness, strained relationships, or personal struggles, God's capacity to heal and restore is limitless. Consider the story of Lazarus: even in death, the power of Christ resurrected him, demonstrating that it is never too late for God to intervene miraculously in our lives.

If you face challenges with your children, health, employment, or education, know that God is not just a distant observer but an active participant in your struggles. He provides not just the bare necessities but abundantly supplies all we need to thrive. His promises are not only for spiritual fulfillment but also for tangible needs and protection in our daily lives.

Ever-Present Help

God's protection is constant; He shields us from seen and unseen dangers. From preventing accidents to providing financially, His hand is evident in every aspect of our lives. More profoundly, He offers solace and companionship during our darkest times, comforting us with His presence when we feel most alone.

The Bible assures us that God is a "present help in trouble" (Psalm 46:1). Therefore, we must rely on Him every moment, knowing that He is our keeper, our protector, and our guide. His vigilance is ceaseless, preserving us from every harm and guiding our every step.

Call to Faithful Reliance

As we navigate the complexities of life, let us continually turn to God, trusting in His infinite wisdom and power. Let us be vigilant in our faith, steadfast in our devotion, and unwavering in our commitment to His will. By doing so, we not only ensure our own spiritual growth but also become vessels through which God can demonstrate His love and power to others.

In every circumstance, let us remember: God is not just our last resort; He is our first and constant source of help. We are called to depend on Him, not out of obligation, but out of a deep understanding of His love for us, manifested supremely through the sacrifice of Jesus Christ on the cross. This sacrifice ensures our eternal safety and His perpetual presence in our lives.

God allow the fiery trials of life refine us, just as gold is purified through fire. This purification process is meant to strip away the impurities and bring out a clearer, stronger faith in us. Thus, when we emerge from these trials, we are not only survivors; we are more resilient, more committed, and more dependent on His grace.

It is crucial for us to recognize that our struggles are not just random misfortunes but are, in fact, part of a divine plan. They are opportunities for growth, designed by God to strengthen our character and deepen our trust in Him. Each challenge we overcome is a testament to His enduring presence and support in our lives.

In embracing this perspective, we can move beyond mere endurance of our trials. We begin to perceive them as blessings in disguise, each one an invitation from God to draw closer to Him and to fortify our faith. This shift in understanding is essential for any believer who wishes to not just go through life but grow through life.

Therefore, as followers of Christ, it is our duty and privilege to rely not on our own strength but on the power provided by the Holy Spirit. He equips us to face every difficulty with courage and to emerge victorious, bearing witness to the mighty work of God in our lives.

Let us hold fast to the promise that "we are more than conquerors through Him who loved us" (Romans 8:37). This assurance empowers us to face each day with hope and boldness, knowing that our victory over trials is guaranteed through Christ. Our faith, once tested, becomes the testimony that inspires others to trust in the transformative power of God's love.

As we continue this journey, let us remember that our ultimate victory is not determined by our ability to avoid challenges but by our decision to face them head-on with Christ at our side. With Him, no obstacle is insurmountable, and no trial is without purpose. Our lives, marked by both trials and triumphs, are a continuous testament to His faithfulness and our enduring faith.

Jesus Christ is the maker of a new covenant with eternal life in Him. He is the source of living water springing up into life everlasting. Thus, Christ sacrificed His life for His sheep who were lost in the darkness of sin. As you, the reader, confront your current challenges, rest assured that God is fully aware of your predicament. You may feel your life is irreparably tangled—that not even God can mend it. Yet, remember, He has allowed these circumstances to unfold.

God stands as your immediate support in times of need. He anticipated these troubles long before the universe and beyond were shaped, before its vast expanse was measured. The sovereign God deeply understands your dire situation. All you need to do is trust Him completely, for He is a miracle worker. Believe firmly that God rewards those who diligently seek Him through His Word and prayer. The trials you endure now are meant to strengthen your faith, to witness God's actions on your behalf.

It's worth reiterating what the Word of God proclaims—that through Christ, who empowers us, we can accomplish all things. Romans 8:28 reinforces this: "And we know that all things work together for good to those who love God, to those who are called according to His purpose."

Too often, Christians are immobilized by needless fear—a force that undermines faith and stifles progress. In the Garden of Gethsemane, had Jesus succumbed to the dread of crucifixion, the salvation plan would have faltered at its inception. However, Christ wholly relied on and trusted in

God the Father, fulfilling the divine plan to bring salvation to humanity. He knew His resurrection was assured by the Father. Likewise, we must place our full trust in God, confident that He will deliver us from evil and guide us through life's tempests.

Fear, a tool of Satan, thrives on the excuses we fabricate to avoid advancing in life. Instead of retreating in the face of trials, we must trust in God for the courage and resilience imparted by the Holy Spirit. Christ set an example by facing every challenge without evasion. He boldly confronted the religious authorities, challenging their interpretations and practices. As followers of Jesus Christ, we must emulate His fortitude and proceed in the direction He guides us, eschewing excuses.

God assures us that while tribulations are inevitable, they do not define us. Christ wants us to recognize that He overcame all life's trials, not to be daunted by them but to triumph over them. His purpose, as discussed in this book, was to vanquish sin and its influence, achieved through His death and resurrection, thereby disarming Satan and his schemes.

Thus, we, too, can conquer every temptation and adversity through the Holy Spirit's power within us. We belong to Christ, not to our adversaries. Without tests, there would be no testimonies. Our testimonies are proof that we have withstood life's adversities and challenges through our faith in Jesus Christ, our Lord. Our hope is anchored solely in Him, to accomplish for us what we cannot.

Every test we encounter is an opportunity to grow our faith and trust in Him. God doesn't introduce trials into our lives to harm us but to strengthen us and propel us toward our destiny. He has already provided a way of escape from every challenge through Jesus Christ. Remember, the battles we face are not ours alone—they belong to the Lord (2 Chronicles 20:15). Trust in God and His Word, and offer Him the highest praise, for He alone is worthy of our gratitude.

God has equipped us not with a spirit of fear, but of power, love, and a sound mind (2 Timothy 1:7 and Philippians 2:5). We are troubled on every side yet not distressed; perplexed but not in despair; persecuted but not forsaken; struck down but not destroyed (2 Corinthians 4:8–9). These words remind us that God sustains us, ensuring we do not falter along the way. Even if we fall, we shall rise, steadfast in our fellowship with God, our ever-present help.

As the children of God, let us bear the fruit of the Spirit, demonstrating through our lives the essence of our faith. We are known by our fruit that is borne from whatever seeds we sow in this life, just as a tree is recognized by its yield. God's directive to be fruitful and multiply was not merely about increasing in number but about flourishing in spiritual abundance, replicating the goodness He planted within us.

In conclusion, let your light shine brightly before others, that they may see your good deeds and glorify your Heavenly Father (Matthew 5:16). Do not hide your light; instead, lift God's name high, allowing Him to work through you for His glory, and in return, He will richly bless your life. My hope is that you, the reader, are drawn into God's Word the Bible and know who He is by diligently seeking Him with the gift of faith. Whoever you are, know that the God of the universe and beyond and who fills every space is laser focused on you to answer His call to repentance and accept eternal life through salvation with His gift of faith which is by Jesus Christ. For there is nowhere in the infinite cosmos that God is not there. He is Jehovah Shamma-the Lord is there (Ezekiel 48:35).

CHAPTER 19

THE JUDGMENT OF GOD

"They went out from us, but they were not of us; for if they had been of us, they would no doubt have continued with us: but they went out, that they might be made manifest that they were not all of us". (1 John2:19). This is a pivotal scripture given to us by John in his first letter to the church. This is showing us that all who sit in pews, officiate in the priest office or in any office of the church are not necessary the true children of God. But they are the tares which grew together with God's true children, the wheat (Matthew 13:24-52). This is the parable that Jesus told concerning the true and false church.

In this pivotal time, as the end approaches, it is crucial for each believer to understand and accept the serious responsibility of being God's watchmen. As watchmen, we are tasked not with living a life that honors God but also with sounding the alarm, alerting both the faithful and the faithless to the impending divine judgment. This role requires vigilance, courage, and unwavering faith in the Word of God.

The urgency of this task cannot be overstated. As the day of the Lord approaches—unexpectedly, like a thief in the night—the scriptures vividly describe a cataclysmic end: the heavens disappearing with a roar, the elements destroyed by fire, and the earth and everything done in it laid bare (2 Peter 3:10). This graphic depiction is not meant to instill fear but to awaken a sober awareness of the finality and the severity of God's judgment.

In the Epistle of Jude, the warning is clear. Those who indulge in sin and reject God's salvation face a dire future. Jude's message serves as a call to all believers to build themselves up in their most holy faith, praying in the Holy Spirit, and maintaining themselves in God's love as they await the mercy of our Lord Jesus Christ, which leads to eternal life.

It is through these spiritual disciplines—prayer, faith, and love—that believers can remain steadfast, despite the challenges and temptations of the world. Moreover, these practices empower believers to distinguish themselves from those who, although they may appear to belong to the faith, are in truth agents of disruption and discord within the church. As John points out, these individuals are like the many antichrists who have arisen, revealing themselves by departing from the fellowship of true believers.

The distinction between those truly of God and those who are not is critical. It is not merely a matter of doctrinal differences but a fundamental divide in allegiance and purpose. Those who are truly God's children will persist in their faith, rooted and grounded in love, continually seeking to align their lives with God's will.

As we consider our role as watchmen, let us also remember the profound grace that has been extended to us. For some, it was a dramatic rescue from imminent destruction, a salvation born out of fear and a loathing for the sin-stained garments of our past. For others, it was God's gentle compassion that drew us away from the brink of eternal separation from Him.

Thus, our message to the world and to each other must be one of urgency and compassion. We must tirelessly work to ensure that no one remains ignorant of the stakes—eternal life with God or eternal separation in destruction. It is a somber task, but it is also a privilege to serve as heralds of the hope and salvation that come through our Lord Jesus Christ.

By maintaining vigilance, living in holiness, and embodying the love of Christ, we fulfill our divine mandate as watchmen for God's kingdom, entrusted with the critical task of warning and guiding others towards the path of salvation. Let us hold fast to this call, knowing that our labor is not in vain, and that through our faithful witness, many may come to know the mercy and grace of our Savior.

This passage reinforces the profound responsibility that falls upon believers, particularly those who act as watchmen. As watchmen, the children of God are tasked with the solemn duty to alert others to the realities of sin and the certainty of divine judgment. This role, deeply embedded in the teachings of the Bible, underscores a critical aspect of Christian duty: the obligation to preach repentance and to offer the hope of salvation to all.

As watchmen, when we fulfill our duty by warning the wicked, we absolve ourselves of responsibility for their choices, as outlined in Ezekiel 33. This Biblical reference is a stark reminder of the consequences of our actions: if we fail to warn others, we share in the guilt of their unrepentant sins; but if we do warn them and they do not turn from their ways, we are not held accountable for their fate.

This emphasizes the necessity of delivering God's message with integrity and compassion. Christ's own mission was marked by mercy and sacrifice—He died for a sinful humanity that rightfully deserved judgment. This act of ultimate love and sacrifice serves as the foundation for our approach to evangelism. We are called not only to speak of judgment but to do so with a spirit of love that reflects Christ's character.

The Great Commission, as stated in Matthew 28:19–20, extends this responsibility to all corners of the globe. It compels us to teach, baptize, and nurture believers in the understanding that Jesus Christ is the singular source of salvation—the only path to reconciliation with God. The urgency of this mission is underlined by the promise of Jesus's constant presence, "even unto the end of the world."

The dire consequences for those who reject this salvation are clear. As Ezekiel 18 and other scriptures assert, each individual bears responsibility for their actions and their ultimate fate in the judgment. God, in His justice, does not delight in the death of the wicked but desires their repentance and salvation. This divine preference for redemption over judgment highlights the critical role of God's messengers in conveying the possibility of forgiveness and a new life through Christ.

The depiction of the final judgment in Revelation and 2 Corinthians illustrates the seriousness with which God regards our lives and choices. Each person will be judged fairly, with the righteous rewarded and the wicked facing punishment, emphasizing that no one is exempt from God's impartial judgment.

As we continue to serve as God's watchmen, let us be motivated by both the fear and love of the Lord. Knowing the "terror of the Lord," we persuade others not out of mere obligation but driven by a genuine concern for their eternal well-being. This dual awareness of God's justice and mercy should guide our efforts, ensuring that our message is not only one of warning but also of hope.

In conclusion, our role as believers and watchmen is to embody the truth of the Gospel in both word and deed. We must diligently work to ensure that all understand their opportunity for salvation through Jesus Christ. By doing so, we fulfill our highest calling to reflect God's love and to offer every person the chance to choose eternal life over eternal separation. This mission, while daunting, is the essence of our faith and the core of our service to God and humanity.

This passage from Romans describes a profound moral and spiritual decay, emphasizing the consequences of turning away from God and pursuing a life led by sinful desires. This scripture illustrates the stark contrast between the lives of the righteous and the wicked, highlighting the divergent paths and their eventual outcomes.

In divine judgment, God does not merely assess the external actions but examines the heart's intentions, thoughts, and the deeds hidden from human eyes. Everything is exposed before God; nothing remains secret. For the righteous, their righteousness is not inherent but is attributed to them through faith in Christ Jesus. The righteousness of Christ covers them, and His blood cleanses their sins. This cleansing is not just a one-time event but a continuous process where the righteous live in obedience to God, constantly realigning with His will through repentance and renewal by the Holy Spirit.

The true children of God are marked by a responsiveness to the Holy Spirit. When they falter and sin, they do not attempt to conceal their wrongs but confess and forsake them, guided by the conviction of the Holy Spirit. This openness to correction and willingness to submit to God's authority are hallmarks of a life transformed by grace.

On the other hand, the wicked are depicted vividly in Romans as those who reject God's truth and exchange it for lies, worshiping the creation rather than the Creator. Their lives are characterized by a series of deliberate choices to ignore the warnings of conscience and the invitations to repentance extended by God. The description in Romans serves as a cautionary tale about the spiritual and moral degradation that follows when individuals persistently reject God's truth.

God's response to persistent rebellion is eventually to "give them over" to their desires, which leads to deeper sin and ultimately to a hardened heart. This judicial abandonment is not God's initial response but a last resort after all avenues for repentance and redemption have been exhausted. The Apostle Paul's words serve as a sobering reminder that persistent sin can lead to a point where a redemptive change becomes nearly impossible, not because of any limitation on God's part, but due to the sinner's continuous rejection of His mercy.

The fruit of the Spirit—love, joy, peace, patience, kindness, goodness, faithfulness, gentleness, and self-control—stand in contrast to the works of the flesh. Those who belong to Christ have crucified the flesh with its passions and desires. Living by the Spirit, they manifest qualities that reflect their divine transformation and alignment with God's will.

In conclusion, as we reflect on these truths, it is crucial for every believer to continually examine their lives in light of Scripture and the Holy Spirit's guidance. The call to live a life characterized by the fruit of the Spirit is not just an ideal but a daily commitment to walk in the newness of life granted through Christ. By so doing, believers not only ensure their alignment with God's will but also bear witness to the transformative power of the Gospel in a world marred by sin and rebellion.

The biblical passages highlight the stark realities and consequences of living in sin without seeking redemption through Jesus Christ. These scriptures serve to remind believers and non-believers alike of the seriousness of God's laws and the finality of His judgment.

1 Corinthians 6:9-10 categorically lists behaviors that are incompatible with inheriting the Kingdom of God, emphasizing that living in such sins without repentance will lead to exclusion from paradise. This is not merely a warning but a declarative statement about the spiritual laws governing righteousness and sin. The passage challenges the notion that one can live in opposition to God's commands and still expect to receive His eternal blessings.

The role of the law, as described in Romans and Psalms, is not only to expose sin but also to lead individuals to a realization of their need for God's salvation. The law serves as a "schoolmaster" to bring us to Christ, showing us our inadequacies and driving us to seek forgiveness and redemption through Him. It highlights the perfection of God's standards and our inability to meet them through our efforts, underscoring the necessity of Christ's sacrificial atonement for our sins.

The scriptural exhortations to separate from the ways of the world and the practices of the unsaved are calls to holiness and purity in a believer's life. As noted in Ephesians, believers are to live differently from those without God, marked by understanding and newness of life in Christ. This differentiation is not just behavioral but transformative, affecting the mind and heart.

Hell, as the ultimate consequence of unrepentant sin, serves as a solemn warning. It was originally prepared for Satan and his angels, but it also becomes the destiny for those who reject God's offer of salvation through Christ. The imagery of being joined to sin as one is joined to a harlot illustrates the complete identification with sin that leads to eternal separation from God.

Finally, the reflections on God's judgment reinforce that it is comprehensive and inescapable. It examines not just outward actions but the intentions of the heart. Those who continue in sin, despite knowing the truth, store up wrath for themselves on the day of judgment. The opportunity to repent is a gift of God's kindness and patience, intended to lead individuals away from sin.

This understanding compels believers to reflect on the gravity of their actions and the world around them. It urges a lifestyle that is in constant alignment with God's will and offers a message of urgency for evangelism. Believers are called to witness to the truth of Christ's redemption, hoping that many will turn from sin and embrace the gift of eternal life through Jesus Christ. This mission is motivated by the love of God and a deep desire to see no one perish but come to repentance and knowledge of the truth.

This scriptural passage underscores a profound truth: while the temporal world and all its glory are fleeting, the Word of God endures eternally, offering salvation and the promise of an everlasting kingdom to those who accept and adhere to it. The message from 1 Peter about the enduring nature of God's Word contrasts sharply with the transient nature of human achievements and life itself. This comparison serves as a potent reminder of what ultimately holds value and permanence.

The long-suffering and patient character of God as described in 2 Peter 3:9 reflects His desire for all to come to repentance rather than perish. It highlights the universal scope of God's mercy, emphasizing that His patience serves as an opportunity for salvation rather than an endorsement of sin. The impending day of the Lord, a theme echoed throughout the New Testament, serves as a critical wake-up call for humanity, marking the culmination of God's plan for the world and the final judgment where all that is tainted by sin will be irreversibly purged.

Matthew 24:14 broadens this perspective by pointing out that the Gospel will reach every corner of the earth before the end times, ensuring that no one can claim ignorance of God's offer of salvation. This global evangelistic outreach underscores the inclusiveness of God's saving grace but also the definitiveness of the ensuing judgment for those who choose to reject it.

The passages from 1 Peter reflect on the persecution and suffering that Christians may face in their temporal lives, positioning these hardships within the broader context of divine justice. The suffering of the faithful is not only seen as part of the Christian experience but is also a purification process, preparing believers for a far greater reward and proving their faith genuine. This suffering contrasts with the final judgment that awaits the ungodly and the sinner, which will be far more sever and terrifying

1 Peter 4:6-7 exhorts believers to live lives marked by vigilance and prayerfulness. The idea that the gospel was preached even to those who are dead reinforces the all-encompassing reach of God's word and the principle that everyone, alive or dead, is subject to God's judgment based on their earthly lives. This again emphasizes the necessity for a righteous life in accordance with God's commandments.

Finally, the parable of Lazarus and the rich man in Luke 16:20-31 serves as a stark illustration of the eternal consequences of earthly actions. It is not a commentary on economic status but a profound lesson on the spiritual repercussions of how we treat others, particularly those in need. The rich man, who lived a life of luxury and indifference towards Lazarus, finds himself in torment in the afterlife, while Lazarus, who suffered on earth, is comforted in the bosom of Abraham. This narrative warns of the dangers of a hardened heart and a life disconnected from the compassionate and righteous demands of God's law.

Together, these passages offer a holistic view of Christian doctrine on judgment and salvation—God's enduring word, His patient call for repentance, the inevitable judgment, and the ultimate separation of the righteous from the wicked based on the choices made in this life. They call for a sober and vigilant life, driven by faith and obedience to God, with an eye toward the eternal implications of our earthly conduct.

Some self-proclaimed "Christians" judge others by their external appearance or social status, overlooking the true character of these individuals. It is simplistic and unhelpful to tell someone to "pick themselves up by their bootstraps." Often, this rhetoric serves to justify our reluctance to share our blessings—blessings which, if acquired justly, are indeed gifts from God. As born-again believers, we should reflect God's generosity through our actions.

True children of God emulate Christ. With the living God within us, our acts of sharing transcend material wealth. They involve imparting the love of Christ and responding to divine inspirations to bless others. Christ taught that if we believe in His works, we are capable of even greater deeds (John 14:12). Thus, we are called to be compassionate witnesses to God's goodness, making a tangible difference in the lives of the less fortunate.

Consider practical ways to assist: tutoring someone in a subject, aiding in GED preparation, assisting with college applications, or guiding someone through the home-buying process. Financial literacy—teaching others to manage debt and make wise investments—can also be transformative. Understanding others' struggles deepens our empathy and motivates us to act as God's hands in their lives.

Regrettably, some Christians misuse judgment, reserved only for God, to justify prejudice and discrimination. This behavior, which distorts the gospel of Jesus Christ and misrepresents His character, is deeply displeasing to God. He urges those who fall into such sin to seek forgiveness and restoration to righteous living. We are no better than those who differ from us; rather, by showing godly love and friendship, we demonstrate the grace that has also saved us.

Our mission is to disciple others, empowered by the Holy Spirit to spread the gospel so that more may be delivered from sin and destruction. As we share our testimonies and the transformative power of God's Word, we remind others of their purpose to glorify God and live victoriously through Christ.

When it comes to judgment, let it be done justly, with grace and mercy, guided by the Holy Spirit and God's Word. Before judging others, we must examine ourselves to ensure we are not hindering their spiritual journey. Understanding that life's challenges can swiftly alter circumstances helps foster compassion rather than judgment.

Every individual faces life's storms—whether natural disasters, political upheaval, or civil unrest—which can devastate lives. In regions like Africa, the Middle East, and Southeast Asia, such turmoil often leaves countless innocent people, including many children, in dire situations due to the greed and cruelty of those in power.

Many victims under oppressive regimes have faced severe religious persecution, particularly from the ruling minorities in certain African countries. These authoritarian leaders mercilessly suppress any opposition, ultimately facing divine judgment for their unrepented sins unless they heed the Holy Spirit's call to repentance. Life can change dramatically in an instant—as exemplified by Job in the Bible—yet it is solely by God's grace that we are spared from His wrath and can partake in His mercy. Jesus's sacrifice was for everyone, demonstrating His universal love.

It is imperative to remember that we have no right to judge others harshly. As Jesus taught, "With the measure you use, it will be measured to you" (Matthew 7:2). If we judge unfairly, we invite unfair judgment upon ourselves. Before correcting others, we must first address our own faults. Practicing the principles of Micah 6:8 will guide us to be truer witnesses of godliness.

As Christians journeying toward Heaven, we must actively spread the gospel of peace. God places people in our lives specifically so we can share the message of salvation. Some may seem beyond help due to the severity of their situations, but God specializes in the impossible. He cleanses and renews, transforming even those most resistant to His word.

God calls us to earnestly pray for these individuals, that their spiritual eyes might be opened and their hearts softened. We are to be God's hands and feet, bringing the gospel to the spiritually lost, not just globally but also locally—including our own homes, often overlooked as mission fields. Living consistently with the Biblical teachings we profess is crucial for effectively witnessing the gospel.

Christians are called to embody Christ's light, showing others what God is like through our lives, which should reflect His virtues of love, kindness, grace, patience, and mercy. We must be compassionate and forgiving, attentive even to the difficult and ungrateful. As co-laborers with Christ, we share the transformative gospel, which turns sinners into saints.

True humility involves walking in the shoes of others as Christ did. He humbled Himself, taking on human flesh, to fully identify with humanity without sinning. This supreme act of love and sacrifice provides the perfect model of godliness for us to follow.

Empowering Salvation Through Service

Every Christian should aspire to save others from the eternal consequence of sin by sharing Christ's gospel. As God's children, we are called to serve the unsaved, hoping that the gospel of Jesus Christ may save them. We should empathize with the backslidden, understanding their circumstances to guide them back to salvation. By relating to the weak and sharing in the pain of the hurting, we aim to draw all closer to Christ, embodying the principle of being "all things to all people" to win them for Jesus (1 Corinthians 9:19-22).

Have you ever wondered why God brought someone unknown and in dire straits into your life? These encounters often teach us humility and servanthood, showing us how to be true neighbors. Our blessings often manifest through being a blessing to others. We don't need to seek out people to help; they are often right next door or among our colleagues. God orchestrates these encounters to give us opportunities to share the life-changing gospel.

Hebrews 13:2 reminds us, "Do not forget to show hospitality to strangers, for by so doing some people have shown hospitality to angels without knowing it." Suspicion and judgment can cause us to miss these divine appointments. Instead, we should pray for God's perspective, as no one is beyond His reach to save from sin.

God has endowed His people with the spirit of discernment, enabling us to distinguish between those seeking to deceive and those He has placed in our paths for a higher purpose. With the blessings we receive from God comes the responsibility to bless others.

I pray that the love of God and the sweet fellowship of the Holy Spirit rest upon you and those you've led to Jesus. For those sincerely seeking transformation, calling upon God can result in profound change, beyond imagination. To every person in the wilderness of unbelief and the desert of skepticism, this book is for you and the living God who desires to welcome you as His child.

Your decision to make Jesus Christ your Lord and Savior today will determine your eternal destiny—whether in the new heavens and new earth or apart from God forever. Choose life with God. Do not disregard the Holy Spirit urging you towards salvation. This moment is all you have.

An encounter with God can forever change your life. By allowing Him to transform us and accept Him as our God, we can anticipate eternal life in heaven. God revives us by infusing our hearts with His Word and igniting our spirits with His own. Let Jesus Christ, the quickening Spirit, illuminate your existence from this moment forward.

Search the Scriptures to discover who God is; He promises to reveal Himself to those who seek Him. Salvation is a divine transaction, not bound by human or church constraints. If you ask Him, God alone will save you from sin. While finding a church that faithfully teaches God's

Word is important, remember that the Holy Spirit is your ultimate guide and teacher. Heaven rejoices when the lost are found and brought into the fold of our Heavenly Father.

The Imminent Return of Christ

Friend, Jesus is coming again, and it may be sooner than we think, especially given the times we are living in. The Bible outlines the events of the end times in Matthew 24, and Revelation details what will happen just before Jesus returns. Revelation 1:7 foretells, "Behold, he cometh with clouds; and every eye shall see him." This momentous return will be witnessed globally, and the righteous who have passed will be resurrected and ascend to meet Him (1 Thessalonians 4:17). This brings us to a crucial question: Where do you stand with Jesus Christ today? Do you truly know Him— not just know about Him—but know Him as your Savior and Lord?

Jesus offers peace and rest from the struggles of a sinful life without requiring anything in return; salvation is a free gift to those who believe He is the only way to God. The Bible urges us to be ready, for Jesus will return at an unexpected hour (Matthew 24:44). Now is the time for salvation. As stated in Deuteronomy 30:19, God has set before us life and death; therefore, choose life, that you and your descendants may live.

The decision is stark and the stakes are high—choose life in Christ, embracing the grace of God (Ephesians 2:8-9), or face eternal separation from God, known as the second death (Revelation 20:14 15). Respond to the Holy Spirit's call to confess and repent. With sincere faith, Jesus will forgive all your sins, granting you eternal life. Commit your life to Him by engaging with His Word, and He will sustain you in perfect peace.

As we anticipate His return, let all who know Jesus walk faithfully, knowing that in the moment of His coming or at the end of our earthly lives, our mortal bodies will be transformed into immortality. I look forward to meeting each of you in heaven. Let us give thanks to God, whose mercy endures forever. Let the redeemed of the Lord say so and await His return in reverent silence.

Acknowledgments and Closing Prayer

Thank you for investing your time in reading this book. I am deeply grateful to God for all of you whose lives have been transformed by the Lord Jesus Christ. There remains an immeasurable number of souls yet to be awakened from spiritual death to new life in God. If you have welcomed

Jesus Christ into your heart through the quickening of the Holy Spirit, you are now His disciple, called to share the good news of eternal life.

It is crucial for every Christian to find and commit to a church that faithfully teaches the Bible's truths. Share this book with someone whose life could be forever changed by the Holy and Sacred Word of God, the Holy Bible.

"Therefore being justified by faith, we have peace with God through our Lord Jesus Christ" (Romans 5:1).

I hope to see each of you in heaven, united with the Eternal God—Father, Son, and Holy Spirit.

REFERENCES

All scripture quotations in this book, unless otherwise noted, are taken from the KJV, NKJV, ASV, NIV.

ABOUT THE AUTHOR

Garfield Cambridge has been a dedicated registered nurse for 27 years, specializing as a pediatric intensive care unit nurse. Raised in Brooklyn, New York, he relocated to the Baltimore area in 1998 with his wife, Natanya, and their children after accepting a position at a renowned hospital in Baltimore, Maryland. Beyond his professional role, Garfield is an elder at his local church in Reisterstown, Maryland.

A devoted husband and father of four, Garfield's passions extend into reading and discussing books on biblical topics and world history. His greatest joy, however, comes from sharing the gospel of salvation through Jesus Christ with those he encounters, guided by his deep conviction that Jesus is the sole source of salvation and eternal life. Garfield believes in the transformative power of the gospel to provide peace on earth and ultimately, a relationship with the God of the Bible.